BOTH SIDES OF THE COIN
THE ARGUMENTS AGAINST THE EURO

Is European monetary union going to usher in a new era of prosperity for Europe or will it precipitate financial meltdown? What will be the effect of euro on jobs? And on interest rates and mortgages?

The single currency fills the pages of the newspapers every day, but the arguments against the euro are never set out clearly and concisely. Here, in an elegant essay by one of Britain's leading economists, are the powerful arguments for remaining outside the single currency. James Forder lucidly explains the arguments against the euro – deflationary pressure, high risk of failure, small upside and its anti-democratic management – and he shows why the advantages have been overstated.

James Forder makes the case against joining the euro persuasively and convincingly.

For the arguments for, turn this book over.

BOTH SIDES OF THE COIN

THE ARGUMENTS AGAINST THE EURO

by

James Forder

P

PROFILE BOOKS

First published in Great Britain in 1999 by
Profile Books Ltd
58A Hatton Garden
London EC1N 9LX

Typeset in Galliard by MacGuru
macguru@pavilion.co.uk
Printed in Great Britain by Biddles Ltd

A CIP catalogue record for this book is available from the British Library.

ISBN 1 86197 107 9

Contents

The author

James Forder is a Fellow of Balliol College, Oxford, where he teaches economics, and senior tutor of the Oxford University Business Economics Programme. His previous publications include *The European Union and National Macroeconomic Policy*, edited with Anand Menon, which considered the evolution of economic policymaking in the European Union, and other essays on European economics and central bank independence. He always thought of himself as a Euroenthusiast until the Maastricht Treaty came to dominate European politics and made this position impossible for a liberal economist.

Preface and acknowledgements

This book is an argument about the most important political decision facing Britain today. With 11 countries adopting the euro on January 1st 1999 the debate will not go away. It has already split the Conservative Party, and it is a defining issue which has the ability to reshape old loyalties. In this context there has been a lot of low political debate, which has largely used whatever projectiles happen to be at hand. But there has been too little elucidation of the economic issues, although there could hardly be anything more economic than the decision on whether to adopt a new currency. We aim to fill the gap.

We have embarked upon the book in this form – in two halves, with a case for and a case against – to highlight the issues behind the decision. Although this is a polemic, it is also designed to ensure that any intelligent reader of a British newspaper is able to cut through the chaff in the debate and focus on the important points. We have, however, imposed certain rules on ourselves. The facts cited on each side in this book are not in dispute between us. What clearly differentiates us are matters of judgment; how much weight should be given to one factor or another.

Books of this kind owe a great debt to others which have gone before. Thanks are also due to colleagues who directly and indirectly helped to shape some of these arguments. Chris Huhne thanks Michael Emerson, with whom he wrote a previous book on the single currency dealing with the general arguments applicable to Europe as a whole. He would also like thank specifically John Arrowsmith, Andrew Duff, Will Hutton, Richard Portes, Lionel Price, Vicky Pryce and William Wallace for reading part or all of the manuscript and for providing many helpful comments and insights. James Forder would like to thank John Arrowsmith, Donna Bellingham, Ann Branch, Anand Menon, Malcolm Walter and, in particular, Peter Oppenheimer for reading the manuscript. They have helped both to excise many errors of fact and interpretation and to substitute clarity for muddle. Any problems that remain are, of course, ours.

James Forder and Christopher Huhne
December 1998

1 Introduction and summary

Euroscepticism is no longer the preserve of nationalists, eccentrics and little-Englanders but has become a cause for the liberal conscience. The Maastricht Treaty has created a monetary union which poses great threats to the prosperity, unity and internationalism of the European Union and to the stability of its member states. The Treaty is based on bad economics and on the foolish view that a common money will promote harmony, irrespective of its management and regardless of its economic consequences.

It is a tragedy that the European Union has adopted this plan, but we cannot help it and probably could never have. There is nothing for us to do now except stand aside from it and avoid embroiling ourselves in Europe's mistake. Britain will then be standing aside, not because of a hallucination of national superiority, or a fatal desire for independence in an interdependent world, or an inflated vision of the importance of our history, language or culture. We shall be standing aside because political ideology should not overrule economic sense; because of a concern that a balance of economic objectives be pursued, not just those of certain interests; and because of a sense of the vulnerability of liberal, democratic and internationalist institutions – European and national – to economic failure.

There is no doubt that the goal of economic and monetary union (EMU) began as the best of European objectives. It was a dream, perhaps a fantasy, but the aim was for unity, internationalism, prosperity and justice. All these were to be promoted, not just symbolised, by the common currency. The first plan for EMU, known as the Werner Plan, made an unfortunate commitment to achieving monetary union by 1980. The plan failed and the embarrassment of missing this target still plays on many minds to the detriment of good judgement. The next attempt to move towards monetary co-operation, the European Monetary System (EMS), began operating in 1979. It functioned well for several years, reducing the short-term volatility of both exchange rates and interest rates, without any particular need for a common currency being perceived.[1]

By the end of the 1980s European prospects seemed excellent. Growth of the European economies seemed likely to speed up and unemployment to fall after a protracted period of inflation-fighting earlier in the decade. There was a new consensus on the right way to conduct economic policy, based on low inflation and sound finance, which many people expected to bring sustained prosperity. The collapse of communist regimes was widely expected to create a great investment opportunity and itself to be likely to further economic growth and political integration in Europe. There also appeared to be a new prospect of faster and deeper European integration. Rapid progress was being made towards the implementation of the 1992 single market project; Britain joined the EMS; and slightly later, after a change of prime minister, the British government even professed itself to be seeking to be 'at the heart of Europe'. It was in this environment that a new plan for monetary union, the Maastricht Plan, based on central bank independence, price stability and low government borrowing was agreed, with initially only Britain standing aside from a full commitment to joining by 1999 at the latest.

Since then things have been more difficult. A rapid acceleration of growth did not materialise. Indeed, unemployment rates began to rise again from already high levels. East European reform was not the immediate success that had been hoped. Inflation remained low, but government finances deteriorated markedly, creating doubt in many minds as to whether the monetary union plan should be implemented. It had been made a condition of participation that countries have low enough government borrowing – less than 3% of national output – and a low enough volume of debt outstanding – less than 60% of national output. As the 1990s progressed many countries seemed likely to miss these targets. Eventually, it was decided that all countries except Greece were 'moving in the right direction', and by virtue of this, rather than of having arrived, were qualified to join. By this time Denmark had decided against joining, and of three new members of the European Union (Sweden, Finland and Austria) Sweden also chose to wait. Thus 11 countries remained eligible and committed when the final decisions were taken and it was decided to proceed.

Much of the distress of the European economies in this period is attributable to German unification, German monetary union and the policies which followed. Nevertheless, events have demonstrated the deficiencies of the Maastricht Plan. Unification took place before Maastricht, but it had been expected to create great investment opportunities and therefore to be on the whole economically beneficial. The outcome was rather different. The Bundesbank chose to regard a small rise in prices as a major threat to economic stability and began raising interest rates. This contributed to what became a long and deep recession in Germany, accompanied by spiralling government debt and the highest unemployment rate Germany has experienced since the Great Depression. German monetary union is not really a good test of the desirability of EMU since a number of the circumstances are different. But the outcome is certainly not a good omen either.

Most of the other EU member states felt forced to raise their interest rates as well, although they were, on the basis of their own economies, in need of lower rates not higher ones. The reason they did this is that higher interest rates in Germany make Deutschemark assets more attractive to investors, leading to the purchase of Deutschemarks and the sale of other currencies.[2] If this had been allowed to occur on a sufficient scale it would have forced the devaluation of the other currencies or, equivalently, the upward valuation of the Deutschemark. The French, in particular, were unwilling to devalue the franc and preferred therefore to see France as well as Germany in deeper and deeper recession. This is the origin of the great, prolonged European recession of the 1990s. It lies in the policy response to German unification in Germany and in the rest of continental Europe. It is no easy matter to pin down just why this policy was followed, but three different stories are told.

The first is simply that the Maastricht Treaty and associated 'gentlemen's agreements' obliged the countries concerned to keep their exchange rates fixed. If so, it is a good demonstration of how easy it is for the European Union to get itself into a position where a serious economic problem arises that the political process cannot readily fix; how political momentum can dominate good economics; and how dangerous it is to suppose that things will inevitably be worked out for the best when commitments have been made to the contrary.

The second story is that French policymakers believed that any devaluation of the franc would inevitably lead to inflation in France, and the rest of continental Europe took France's lead. This argument is not correct since the change in the French price level depends on the level of unemployment in France as well as the exchange rate. Devaluations in recessions, when accompanied by other appropriate policies, have been extremely effective in restoring prosperity without raising inflation to any significant extent. Britain in 1992 is an obvious example. There are also examples of failed devaluations, such as the French ones of 1981 and 1983. But they failed, leading to inflation, because they were accompanied by other policies which were themselves inflationary at a time when the opposite was required.

The third story is that French policymakers feared for their credibility. That is, it was not the devaluation itself that was thought undesirable, but rather the demonstration of a willingness to devalue. Currency markets, so the argument runs, would forever expect that further devaluations were imminent and the franc would be bedevilled by permanent speculation. This argument has been shown to be nonsense by the British experience since 1992. An initial devaluation was not met by continuing speculation on further falls. Indeed, it was not long before a rising, not a falling, pound became the problem. Nevertheless, the doctrine of credibility continues to have a powerful influence on European thinking. The suspicion that this was at least part of the reason the French chose damaging interest-rate increases rather than an appropriate devaluation should also be a warning that although policymakers are concerned with their credibility, this consideration can appear to be a justification for all kinds of foolish policy.

Meanwhile, Britain, having joined the exchange-rate mechanism of the EMS in 1990 after years of dispute within the government, also found itself with an overvalued currency. Many jobs were lost and much money spent in the attempt to maintain the rate with the same persistent references to the importance of credibility from the chancellor of the exchequer, Norman Lamont. Ultimately, it proved impossible and devaluation and a much-improved economy followed. It is a pity that devaluation did not come earlier, but at least it came, in contrast to France.

These developments should in themselves demonstrate the folly of EMU. A policy was adopted in Germany that was quite simply inappropriate for France, Britain, Italy and the rest of the EMS. This is the key cost of a single currency: that every member country must have the same interest rate regardless of its circumstances. No one need look further for an example of the damage EMU can do: the developments following German unification are a perfect case.

In Britain advocates of the euro argue that our EMS experience shows nothing because we joined at the wrong time, when the pound was overvalued. This may be true, but there are few advocates of British membership of the euro now who were not advocates of the EMS in 1990, and at that time they had as little patience with the view that the time was not right as they do today with the same argument about the euro. In any case, this view offers no kind of answer to the question of what caused the great European recession. The other countries had been in the EMS for years.

In France, however, a more important mistake has been made. This is to suppose that the problems of the French economy would have been avoided if there had been joint control over monetary policy in the EMS, rather than everyone in practice following the lead of the Bundesbank. From this perspective EMU solves the problem, since it means there will be international control over policy. There are two things wrong with this. One is that the EMS was itself explicitly designed to be symmetric; that is, there would be no one country leading the system. This idea evidently came to nothing, so it is not at all clear that a second attempt will be more successful.

Moreover, this solution is no solution at all from the point of view of Europe as a whole. Certainly, the problem faced by the French was that they found themselves in the position where the Germans were setting policy. But, on the assumption that this policy was the best for Germany, having someone else set policy, such as an international committee of bankers as the Maastricht Treaty does, can make policy better for France only by making it worse for Germany. Fundamentally, what German unification demonstrates is not the cost of having German policy applied throughout Europe, but the cost of having any single policy applied. This policy could have been more favourable to the rest of Europe, but only by being less like the policy the Germans desired. No doubt in future it will be seen as a great irony that EMU came to be regarded as urgent in reaction to events which demonstrated its undesirability.

It can be said, in defence of EMU, that German unification was a one-off event, never to be repeated, but it is a frail defence. It is in the nature of events dangerous to Euroland that they are unpredictable. Unification is merely an example of the kind of problem that can arise, and when it does arise is serious. Different circumstances in different countries lead to a desire for different policies, but a monetary union forces us all to have the same policy.

A further lesson can be drawn from the experience of the whole of Europe, including Britain, since the early 1980s. Around that time it became fashionable in economic policymaking circles to suppose that inflation is the only true economic evil. If only inflation could be controlled, it was supposed, and price stability achieved, everything else would fall into place. Unemployment would look after itself, and the forces of the market would deliver rapid economic growth and prosperity. Certainly, an emphasis on the control of inflation was appropriate in many countries for much of the 1980s, but it is now clear that the wider promise has not been fulfilled.

The crucial point is that unemployment does not 'look after itself' and return to a low level once inflation has been eliminated. Long and deep recessions lead to unemployment levels more or less permanently higher than before. This means that policymakers cannot afford to think only in terms of the control of inflation. They must recognise other objectives as quite proper as well.

Unfortunately, in 1991 the Maastricht Treaty was written to enforce the policy presumptions of that time in the future monetary union. Consequently, the European Central Bank (ECB) is obliged to pursue price stability, whatever the cost in unemployment and growth. It is to be left entirely free of any kind of control in doing this. To make matters worse, the use of fiscal policy (that is, the balance of government taxation and expenditure) is also to be severely restricted so that a potentially important mitigating force will probably be devoid of significant power.

The advocates of EMU are in two minds about how to respond to this point. On one hand, people such as Emerson and others, who were writing on behalf of the European Commission,[3] take the line that the control of inflation is indeed the only proper objective of policy. In this case the unaccountability of the ECB and its exclusive focus on inflation are benefits of the euro. On the other hand, these views are hard to sustain when looking at the actual course of unemployment in Europe. Consequently, others among the advocates of the euro are inclined to say that no one could possibly take the Treaty literally and that the ECB will take a far more balanced view than it suggests and be far more responsive to the European democracies. The difficulty for this group, of course, is what to say about the first group.

Many advocates of integration evidently do believe that the Treaty should be followed to the letter, and this appears to be true of the staff of the ECB itself.

Furthermore, the Treaty plays into the hands of those who would have this policy followed by giving it legal backing. This point is illustrated by the behaviour of the Monetary Policy Committee (MPC) of the Bank of England. Many people have called for lower interest rates and accused the MPC of being insufficiently representative of the regions or industry, or of knowing too little about the real world. Members of the MPC have made many speeches, answering that this is an unfair change because they are simply doing as they are told: trying to achieve a specific inflation outcome as set by the government. There is no reason to think that individuals more representative of industry would be better able to achieve this outcome and therefore, they argue, there is no case to answer. They are right, of course, as far as they go. But the appropriate question is whether they should have been given this task in the first place; whether it might not have been better to recognise that this policy would have undesirable side effects, such as an excessive rise in the value of the pound, doing permanent damage to British exports.

The members of the MPC have not had to address the question of whether their policy is good policy, and have stuck to the claim that it is the policy they have been told to follow. Why would we expect the ECB, which will certainly be much more firmly under the sway of anti-inflationary interests, to take a different view? The ECB will argue that it is legally required to pursue price stability above all other goals, and therefore complaints about its failure to recognise other goals are beside the point. In the British case there is also the possibility of a change of view by the government, which might give a different instruction, although once the commitment to low inflation has been made it is politically difficult to change. In the European case such a change would require a Treaty amendment and can therefore be ruled out. So we should take entirely seriously the view that the Treaty means exactly what it says, and in rejecting the theory on which it is based reject the Treaty too.

So it is easy to see that bad economic policy is likely to be the outcome of EMU. There are two ways for bad policy to arise. One is that different areas need different policy and they cannot have it, so someone has bad policy, or all have a compromise bad policy. Alternatively, the whole area may suffer from an excessively deflationary policy based on the disregard of any economic objective other than price stability.

Politically, poor economic performance is sure to reflect badly on the European ideal. But there is more to it than this simple fact. It is necessary to consider the case of a damaging policy being imposed from a foreign city. Imagine the case where inflation is a problem in Germany, France and some of the other countries. Interest rates rise, leading to a recession in one of the poorer countries which, let us suppose, did not have an inflation problem, and perhaps even needed lower interest rates. Most of the advocates of EMU, who are also hoping for closer political ties, apparently believe that using the same money will bind Europeans together more than the fact that rich countries will be seen to be imposing pointless recessions on poor ones will push them apart. This view is palpably naive. Indeed, it is difficult to see such circumstances leading to anything but a growth of nationalist and perhaps even secessionist political movements in the recession-bound countries.

The fact that the governments of these countries are prohibited from seeking any mitigation of the harmful monetary policy can only make the problem worse. A policymaker who is seen to be accountable to the people of Europe as a whole might have a chance in such circumstances. One like the ECB, which will inevitably be seen as acting in the interest of the moneyed classes of the rich countries, will have none. It can lead only to the loss of legitimacy of European integration and in the extreme to the fragmentation of the Union.

So Maastricht means bad economic policy; this is anybody's case against the euro. But bad economic policy means bad economic outcomes, and when these are seen to be imposed from a foreign city, bad economics quickly becomes bad politics. This is the case for the liberals and internationalists, who have always welcomed European integration, to reject the euro.

2 The advantages of the euro

It is agreed on all sides that there are both costs and benefits of a group of countries sharing a currency. Most of the points that are frequently made either in favour of or against EMU could be made in the case of a proposal for a common currency for any group of countries. The balance of costs and benefits in each case would be different, but their basic character would be the same.

A large number of such benefits have been claimed for EMU. Most of them are ultimately traceable to the saving of costs in international transactions that a single currency brings. This is most obviously the case with the costs of trade, but the costs of dealing with exchange-rate uncertainty can be thought of in this way too. It has also been claimed that the euro will confer some international advantages on the European Union which are not simply the consequence of lower transactions costs. Offering a currency which can challenge the dollar in international markets is supposed to be one of these. Further, and much more speculative, claims have been made that eliminating these costs will itself lead to other gains, such as an improvement in the rate of economic growth on a permanent basis.

However, the economic costs of monetary unions are mainly traceable to the loss of the ability to set different monetary policies in different countries to reflect different conditions or preferences. It is in the nature of a monetary union that all parts of the union will share the same interest rates and the same exchange rate with the rest of the world. As the case of policymaking after German unification has illustrated, there will be circumstances when this forced uniformity is undesirable.

The essence of the case for EMU in Europe is that the benefits outweigh the costs. It is possible that this is indeed the case for a small group of countries within the European Union: not even the most ardent Eurosceptic should rush to argue that Germany and the Netherlands would not be well served by a single currency. It is most unlikely, however, that there are net benefits for all the 15 members, let alone the 15 and the countries of central and eastern Europe and others that are currently hoping to join the European Union. Certainly, there is no reliable measure of these costs and benefits which clearly shows significant gains from such a monetary union.

As well as these arguments, which might apply with small changes to any monetary union, in the European case three other types of arguments have been advanced. First, the European Commission says that 'the better formulation and implementation' of EU policies will bring benefits. However, its argument on this point simply consists of a wish-list of policy areas the Commission would like to control with no reason given for supposing they are linked with monetary union.[4]

Second, the euro is said to have political benefits. This important issue is considered in Chapter 6. The essential point is that if the euro is economically damaging, it is unlikely to promote harmony in the political sphere for long. The matter should therefore be debated in the first instance in terms of economic effects alone.

Third, it has been claimed that certain details of the institutional arrangements of the Maastricht Treaty give rise to extra benefits. In particular, the independent central bank and the Stability and Growth Pact are said to bring such benefits. This is a most serious mistake. It is just these arrangements which create much the most powerful argument against EMU and against British membership. Since these things are costs, not benefits, they will be considered in Chapter 3.

The benefits of a single currency
Saving transactions costs
The most obvious benefit of a single currency is that some transactions costs in international business and travel can be eliminated, namely the

cost of exchanging money when engaging in transactions in other member countries. Besides the benefit to those already involved in international transactions, there will be a few other individuals and companies who will be encouraged by the lower costs to engage in trade, so that there will also be an increase in the total volume of trade, presumably bringing some slight efficiency gain.

No one denies these benefits exist, but what of it? How important are they? The European Commission is far from being a disinterested party, but even its estimate puts the benefits at only 0.4% of EU national income, with a concentration in the smaller and poorer countries.[5] A 0.4% gain would mean that, on average, for every £100 we currently have, EMU brings an extra 40 pence through the elimination of transactions costs. Since the United Kingdom is neither one of the smaller, such as Belgium or Ireland, nor one of the poorer countries, such as Greece or Portugal, the actual benefit might be as little as half of this, again according to the European Commission.

Even this figure needs to be treated with care. The benefit arises from the fact that certain functions no longer need to be performed. These are the functions of exchanging currencies in banks and bureaux de changes around the continent and the related processing ones behind the scenes. The resources, mostly people, formerly employed to perform these functions can therefore, in principle, be employed on some other function. Society as a whole gains the benefit of the performance of that other function. This means that the cost saving identified by the European Commission must initially manifest itself as a loss of jobs in the banking sector, and presumably a loss of profitability in this sector as well. The benefit of monetary union arises only when the resources released from banking actually find alternative employment, which may take some time.

Transparency of pricing

Another benefit claimed by advocates of the euro is the so-called transparency of pricing. It is argued that having prices in a single currency will make it easier for consumers to compare them, and this will force prices down in the countries where they are currently highest, otherwise people will simply import the goods in question from a country where they are cheaper. The outstanding example of the benefits that this would bring is usually held to be the reduction of the price of new cars in Britain, where they are much higher than in continental Europe.

To take this seriously, we must believe that it is specifically the existence of different currencies which allows retailers to get away with charging British buyers substantially more than continental buyers. If this were true, it would have to be the difficulty either of comparing prices or of changing currencies which prevented the British from buying on the continent. Since the potential savings are said to be several thousands of pounds per car, it is difficult to take seriously the idea that this is really the explanation.

An alternative explanation is that car makers and car dealers may be organising a restriction of trade. Indeed, when it was pushing the 1992, or single market, programme the European Commission itself blamed a variety of things, including its own regulations and 'the trading practices of the leading manufacturers' for these price differences, without mentioning the possibility that the existence of different currencies might have anything to do with it.[6] Another possibility is that British consumers have not been sufficiently aware that right-hand drive vehicles can be bought on the continent at continental prices. If one of these things is the explanation, monetary union will not solve the problem. Furthermore, it has now become apparent that there are four-figure price differences for economy cars even within Britain. The *Observer* of November 1st 1998 reported that a Renault Clio priced at £10,715 in Southampton could be bought for £9,750 in Cardiff. A Ford Escort was £12,020 in Plymouth but only £10,650 in Newcastle, and there were other, similar, examples. This surely must show that whatever the cause of price differences between Britain and the rest of Europe, it is not that we have a separate currency.

Reducing exchange-rate uncertainty

A third possible source of benefit from a single currency is the elimination of costs associated with uncertainty about future exchange rates. For example, if a firm is contemplating an investment which will ultimately produce revenue from a foreign country, it may be inhibited by the fact that it does not know what that revenue will be worth in terms of its own currency. This introduces an element of risk into any such investment. If this risk is a serious problem to a sufficiently large number of firms, efficient financial markets might be expected to be able to eliminate it, although of course they would charge a fee. In this case the fee is the cost of the exchange-rate uncertainty. The fact that firms cannot generally purchase this kind of insurance must to some degree suggest that there is not much demand for it. This, in turn, suggests that the perceived risks are not all that great.

It must also be recognised that any gain in lower exchange-rate uncertainty may come at the price of more uncertainty of other kinds. For example, in Chapter 3 it will be argued that unemployment is likely to be less stable in a monetary union, and therefore investment projects in general will be shrouded in more uncertainty as to their likely returns. The mere fact that less exchange-rate uncertainty, if other things are equal, might promote investment does not lead to the supposition that any measures that reduce exchange-rate uncertainty will increase investment, since they will not typically leave other things equal.

Even considering the issue of exchange-rate uncertainty alone, the argument is more problematic than it seems. One issue is the effect of the introduction of the euro on the unpredictability of exchange rates between Europe and the rest of the world. Should this increase, the gains for European businesses trading exclusively in Europe would have to be set against losses to those seeking to trade with the rest of the world. There is, unfortunately, every chance that there will be such a deterioration, since the euro, being a much more important currency than any of the national currencies, is likely to attract rather more speculation than most of them have. This in itself could be a cost of the euro.

Another problem is that it is difficult to detect evidence of costs from exchange-rate uncertainty. Even the European Commission was unable to report any research showing a measurable increase in trade as a consequence of exchange-rate stability, although we can be sure it looked pretty hard.[7] Presumably, this is because any such effect is small, a fact which hardly argues in favour of the euro, however appealing the theory.

It should be noted that in so far as there are, in normal circumstances, benefits in exchange-rate stability, nothing prohibits Britain or any other country outside the euro from pursuing a policy designed to stabilise its exchange rate. Chris Huhne quotes some figures relating to the excessive volatility of the pound in recent years, but the most they show is that more attention should be paid to the stabilisation of the exchange rate as one aspect of a balanced policy.

Challenging the dollar

Creating a currency which can rival the dollar has been one of the long-standing goals of many continental policymakers, although it has never been entirely clear what it means. If it is really a matter of international prestige or 'giving the European Union a monetary identity', we should be cautious as to whether any real benefit exists.

Another possibility is that it is anticipated that the euro will displace the dollar as the currency of pricing of internationally traded goods such as oil. At present, wherever in the world oil is traded it is priced in dollars. It is difficult to see that any national advantage accrues to the United States from this fact. Everybody has to pay the same amount of money whatever currency the prices are quoted in. And if there is some advantage, why would the creation of the euro cause the Americans or anyone else to change the way oil is priced?

Much the same thinking applies to British companies which have announced that they intend to keep certain accounts in euros rather than pounds. They are free to think in whatever currency they like, but nothing material is affected by the decision, and their practices in this regard have no bearing on whether it is beneficial to the country as a whole to adopt the use of a different currency and accept having its monetary policy made abroad.

A slightly more serious idea is that at present the United States gains a benefit from the fact that non-Americans hold dollars rather than their own currency. As a result the US government has what is in effect an interest-free loan. Similar, although smaller, benefits currently accrue to European governments, but it is hoped that the euro will play an international role like that of the dollar to a greater extent than the existing currencies do.

It has been suggested that the issuance of a €500 note will be useful to the mafia around the world, since large amounts of money can be transported easily in this form without having to go through the banking system. It has even been suggested that easing the transactions of the mafia is an objective of issuing these notes. If this is true, it is rather disreputable. It is an unlikely thought that the European Union wishes to be in the business of lubricating the illegal and drug-related activities of the world's mafia by offering them a more convenient store of value than the dollar, but it has to be admitted that a small financial benefit would result.

Although such effects, if they occur, might be counted as a benefit by some, this would still be a difficult area for advocates of the euro. The Bundesbank regarded the accumulation of Deutschemarks abroad as disadvantageous for Germany because it put the Bundesbank in danger of losing control of the German money supply. On this basis challenging the dollar would be seen as a disadvantage.

Lower interest rates

It has also been argued that if Britain joined the euro British interest rates would fall. In the circumstances at the end of 1998 this was clearly true. But it is a mistake to count this as a benefit of the euro. As regards short-term interest rates – those which determine most people's mortgages – the Bank of England currently has the job of setting them, and if they would be changed by joining the euro it would be nice to be able to assume that this would be a change for the worse, otherwise the Bank of England would presumably lower them of its own accord. It is tempting for those with variable-rate mortgages to think that joining the euro area would work in their favour, but it is important to realise that this would come at the expense of mismanagement of the economy with long-term costs for everyone.

Long-term interest rates are usually thought to be determined by market perceptions of likely future rates of inflation and the possibility of a government default. British long-term interest rates have generally been higher than corresponding German rates, which, on the basis that it is assumed neither government will default, would mean that inflation in Britain has been expected to be higher than in Germany. Joining the euro is presented as a way of ensuring that British and German inflation rates will be the same, and therefore of lowering long-term interest rates in Britain.

In tackling this argument, it is important to be clear whether it is being assumed that British inflation actually will be higher than German inflation, or whether it is merely the fear of it that makes interest rates higher. If it is the former, the British government is at no financial disadvantage; what it pays in extra interest it gets back by repaying its debt with inflated money. If this is not the intention, however, and therefore it is merely the markets' groundless fear that debt will be repaid with inflated pounds that causes British interest rates to be higher than German rates, a far less drastic solution than joining the euro is available. The British government already borrows on index-linked terms: that is, it pays inflation plus a certain amount. In this case a lender need have no reason to care what inflation turns out to be since it is the amount of money equal to a specified purchasing power that the government promises to repay. Therefore, if the government feels the markets are taking an unfairly gloomy view of what inflation will be, it could issue more, or even all, of its debt in this way.

Effects on the rate of growth

All of the benefits so far considered offer, if they offer anything, a one-time improvement in the European standard of living. If there are savings from the elimination of transactions costs, the labour and capital released can be used in some other activity. If there are benefits of the reduction of uncertainty, some extra investment may take place. Once these things are done these benefits can be kept, but there is no recurring, additional benefit. The most that can be said for any of these effects is that they might allow us to take a step up, but once this is done they do not allow us to take any further steps upwards which would not have been available in any case.

It is often claimed, however, that in addition to the factors already considered there will be an increase in the rate of growth of the European economy. The argument is made that we have the one-time gains already considered and that these increase output, and it is reasonable to suppose some of this extra output will be saved and invested. If this happens the capital stock grows faster than it otherwise would have and thus increases output further, yielding additional benefits in the form of a faster rate of growth. These are sometimes called dynamic gains. By this argument the advocates of the euro hope to show that small initial benefits can, over time, through the working of compound growth rates, turn into worthwhile amounts of money. Indeed, it is true that if a policy can be devised which will increase the rate of growth, even by a fraction of 1%, large gains will eventually result.

However, to treat this point as it stands as a further argument for the euro is a mistake. A crucial aspect of the argument is that the basic effects of the euro are positive. It must be that there is initially an increase in output to generate the increase in investment, which is the basis of the dynamic gain. But before it can be determined whether this increase in output exists, it is necessary to consider both the costs and the benefits of the euro, not just the benefits. It cannot be argued that the savings in transactions costs will generate extra investment, and that this will bring a dynamic benefit, if the issue of the dynamic costs associated with the harmful effects of the euro is then ignored. The elementary mistake of supposing that dynamic effects can exist only on the benefit side was made by the European Commission and has unfortunately been followed by almost all who have written on the matter since.

So dynamic effects should not feature at all in a discussion of whether the euro is desirable. Once this issue has been settled dynamic effects may change the size of the overall cost or benefit. But then the power of compound growth might just as well be working against the advocates of the euro as in their favour, and it takes only a small negative effect on the growth rate for the dynamic consequences for Europe to be disastrous.

Similar points may be made in relation to other claims that are made for the euro. For example, an old standby of the European Commission is the survey of business opinion. When business opinion is favourable to the Commission's proposals, much is made of the fact that the increased confidence will promote investment.[8] But, again, a favourable opinion cannot be expected to be maintained if the consequences turn out to be negative, and then presumably the same line of argument suggests a dramatic fall in investment.

On the benefit side, therefore, we have very little. The saving in transactions costs, 40p in £100 on average but less in Britain, seems to be the most concrete. There is the essentially speculative issue of whether the balance of reduced exchange-rate uncertainty within Europe and increased uncertainty between Europe and the rest of the world will bring benefits or costs, and, if the former, whether they will be worthwhile benefits in terms of improving economic well-being. Then there is the amorphous issue of challenging the dollar. Other claimed benefits, such as that there will be an equalisation of prices or government interest rates in different countries and that there are significant dynamic benefits, are not, once they are properly considered, relevant.

3 The disadvantages of the euro

O n the cost side, it is important to distinguish between costs which would arise from any introduction of a single currency in an area the size of the European Union and those which arise specifically from the details of the Maastricht Treaty. The overwhelming effort of advocates of the euro has gone into arguing that the European Union would benefit from a single currency, and it is important that the deficiencies of these arguments are appreciated. There has been comparatively little effort to address the serious deficiencies of the Maastricht Treaty, which is not only economically dangerous but also threatens to undermine the political fabric of Europe. This chapter will consider the costs of any single currency and then the details of the Maastricht Treaty.

PART 1 THE COSTS OF A SINGLE CURRENCY

The costs of common policy

The important cost of a single currency is that all parts of the monetary union must have the same monetary and exchange-rate policy at all times. Clearly, if Germany and Spain have the same currency, the exchange rate between the Spanish currency and the dollar and the Germany currency and the dollar must be the same. Similarly, interest rates must be the same in both countries. The case would be the same as in the United States. Interest rates cannot be systematically lower in New York than in California, simply because nothing prevents a Californian borrowing in New York and lending in California, if this is advantageous. Any such transcontinental borrowing would itself tend to lead to an equalisation of interest rates.

Interest-rate differences may exist when there are separate currencies because in this case, even in the absence of legal restrictions on foreign borrowing, people have to be aware of the dangers of changes in currency values. In 1998 a European could borrow at lower interest rates in Japan than anywhere in the European Union. But when the time comes to repay the loan, the number of euros owed will depend on how the exchange rate has changed in the interim. Presumably, it is this danger that has deterred large numbers of Europeans from borrowing in yen. This factor does not exist within a currency union and there is therefore no impediment to the equalisation of interest rates.

There are three cases where it will be disadvantageous to have the same interest rates everywhere. The most frequently discussed is that of non-synchronous business cycles. This is sometimes called the problem of asymmetric shocks, with a shock being anything which causes either a boom or a recession. It is asymmetric if different countries suffer different shocks, or some suffer none at all. In such a case higher interest rates could be called for in one country whereas lower ones are needed in another. This was the problem that arose after German unification. It was also the general pattern in the few years up to the middle of 1998: Britain was recovering from recession and apparently in danger of heading towards a boom, calling for some increase in interest rates; most of continental Europe was stuck in recession and needed lower interest rates. This point alone should convince anyone that the issue of timing of joining the euro is important. At the beginning of 1999 most continental European countries are at broadly the same point in their business cycles, so at least they start off with roughly the same policy desires. This is not true of the United Kingdom, and the idea that our interests would somehow be served by jumping into a monetary union at the beginning with the British economy in a quite different condition from that of the continent is absurd.

Much the same can be said of Ireland, where a boom developed during the latter part of the 1990s. Committed to the Maastricht process, Ireland did not set interest rates in accordance with domestic conditions, but rather sought to follow the rest of Europe. This resulted in interest rates being lower than they otherwise would have been. With Ireland in the euro and forced to accept even lower interest rates, we should expect the boom to get worse and inflation to rise until the Irish economy loses competitiveness sufficiently for a bust to ensue. At this point Ireland will want lower interest rates, and it will have to hope that the continental economy is not at the point of recovery where interest rates are rising. If they are, the Irish recession will be deep and a heavy price will have been paid for allowing political objectives to dominate policy in disregard of the basic economics of the situation.

Another case where a different policy would be desirable in some countries arose late in 1998 when after a fall in commodity prices Norway, a major commodities exporter, found its exchange rate falling. This is desirable. If the price of a major export has fallen sharply, damaging employment, some fall in the currency is an appropriate response. Finland is also a commodities exporter and was in addition subject to the implosion of the Russian economy, but the exchange rate did not fall. The advocates of the euro tried to argue that this showed its benefits: the markets were convinced of Finnish commitment to the euro and so did not attack the currency. But this is a mistake. What the markets did was understand that the commitment of the Finnish government to the euro would prevent a sensible devaluation. But the markets' belief that a commitment to the euro has been made is not the same thing as it being a good idea. Finland should have welcomed a devaluation in response to these external events.

Since the Maastricht Treaty was signed by 12 countries in 1991 we have had three clear cases of a different policy being needed in different countries. One in Germany after unification, one for Britain with a recovery that began in 1992 while the continent languished in recession, and one for Ireland as a consequence, mainly, of the large amount of foreign direct investment that has been occurring and generating a boom there. It should be stressed that these are only the comparatively clear cases, and only the ones relating to the original 12 signatories. The Greek economy is chronically out of step with the rest on many measures, and it is not clear that Portugal has suffered as badly as others from the Euro-recession of the last decade. The Finnish case is another, but Finland was not one of the original 12. Let no one therefore imagine that such cases are rare and that this problem can be brushed aside with the assurance that German unification is a unique event. It may be politically unique, but in economic terms it fits a recurring pattern.

The consequence of events like these is that some countries end up with poor policy. In some cases this will mean they are forced into recession, as France was after German unification; in others it will mean they experience booms, like the Irish one. But the booms, if uncontrolled, will turn to recession as prices rise and competitiveness is lost. When recession develops unemployment rises, firms go bankrupt and economic growth slows. These are the consequences of monetary union. And it is the costs of unemployment, bankruptcy and slow growth which need to be set against the alleged benefits: the 40p in £100 and claims that mortgage payments will be lower in Euroland. Being unemployed does not make paying a mortgage any easier.

There are two other cases, apart from non-synchronous business cycles, when it is desirable to pursue different policies in different countries. One is when different economies respond at different speeds to the same policy. Take, for example, a common problem of inflation, perhaps originating in developments in the rest of the world, such as an oil-price rise. In some countries the initial inflation may be readily perceived as a one-time shock, so it gives rise to little continuing wage pressure. In others, perceptions of continuing inflation may persist longer once it has started. In this case wages and prices will presumably continue to rise faster in the second country than in the first, and a policy that started off as appropriate for both will not remain so for long.

The second possibility is that different countries will have different preferences. In the case of a common rise in inflation, some may prefer its immediate reduction, but others may feel that there will be lower costs in the long run if a more gradual reduction of inflation allows its containment, with a smaller rise in unemployment.

In each of these examples the policy ends up being a compromise of some kind. A small country such as Ireland will more or less have the continent's preferences imposed on it. A larger one may influence the choice of policy, but then the policy serves no interest fully. This is the basic cost of a single currency, whether in Europe or elsewhere.

The benefits of devaluations

A common element of these situations is that in the absence of monetary union they are likely to be met with different interest rates, which will lead to exchange-rate changes. It has been a theme of the advocacy of monetary union that exchange-rate changes cannot bring any benefits beyond, perhaps, the short run. Thus Emerson *et al*.[9] say that after an initial benefit from devaluation 'import prices work through into consumption prices. These price increases will sooner or later feed through in nominal wages and therefore in domestic output prices', so that in the longer term devaluation causes only inflation.

This certainly appears to be true of some devaluations, such as those of the franc in 1981 and 1983. Others, however, have been highly successful. Most obvious among these is the British exit from the ERM in 1992, which clearly restarted growth. Although opponents of devaluation at the time were convinced that there would be high inflation within a year or two, they were wrong. Nor is this exceptional; Belgium enjoyed a successful devaluation in 1982 as did Mexico in 1994. Indeed, even the French devaluations of 1958 and 1968 were successful. The puzzle is why some devaluations are successful and others are not.

It is easy to see the effects of a devaluation in a country with full employment as inflationary. The devaluation improves the competitiveness of both exporting and import-competing firms by reducing the amount of foreign currency required to pay a price fixed in the domestic currency. When the pound was devalued each Deutschemark bought more pounds, so from the German point of view British exports became cheaper. Similarly, from the British point of view more pounds were needed to purchase imports.

These effects have two inflationary tendencies. One is that imports cost more. Whether these are final goods or inputs to production, the price to consumers in the devaluing country will generally be higher. The other is that the improvement in competitiveness will increase employment, and this too will push in the direction of higher wages and hence higher costs and prices. If, as assumed, the devaluing country has full employment, an increase in inflation must be expected. There is a greater demand for labour but few unemployed workers. Presumably there was already buoyant consumer demand and retailers will feel free to raise prices. If the devaluation also comes at time of expansionary government policy, as it may since this policy may be the reason for the low level of unemployment, there is further reason to expect a rapid price increase.

The case is different for a country that has been pursuing an anti-inflation policy but finds its currency overvalued, perhaps because of past inflation. The country will be experiencing a recession and unemployment will presumably be rather high because of the anti-inflationary policy and because the past inflation will have put domestic firms at a competitive disadvantage to foreign ones. It is reasonable to hope that the improved competitiveness following a devaluation will result in a fall in unemployment, and that prices will be slower to rise. The devaluation still creates some tendency to inflation, but this simply shows why successful devaluations have tended not only to occur with unemployment rather high, but also to be accompanied by continued disinflationary policy.

Confusion arises because advocates of the euro, among others, speak as if the successful outcome of the British devaluation of 1992 was merely a piece of luck. They imply that recession, lack of consumer confidence, the high level of unemployment and the continued government policy of bearing down on inflation were just a fortunate coincidence. The truth is that it is precisely such circumstances which make devaluation an appropriate weapon. No one would have been advocating a devaluation had these not been the circumstances. Similar situations may be expected to arise in some part of the European Union fairly frequently. If the circumstances are right and the accompanying policies are appropriate there is no reason all devaluations should not be successful.

Advocates of the euro are also inclined to assert that most British devaluations have led only to inflation and that there has been some sort of vicious circle at work. The record since the second world war is as follows. In 1949 there was a general European devaluation against the dollar in which Britain played a leading role, but which involved the whole continent. It did much to balance the post-war world economy, and there was no appreciable inflation subsequently. Next came a highly successful devaluation in 1967. Some years later there was a major inflation, the 'Barber boom', but this was caused by a quite separate mishandling of policy by a later government. In 1971 there was a general realignment of the Bretton Woods system, again not focusing on Britain. The major feature was a devaluation of the dollar, and the value of the pound increased in dollar terms. In 1972 Britain left the European snake and the pound floated (downwards). This occurred in inflationary conditions and would not be expected to bring any benefits: this one case roughly fits the alleged general pattern. Lastly, in 1992, there was the exit from the EMS and another float, which has been extremely successful. Indeed, I would argue that the British problem has been one of excessive resistance to devaluation and consequent persistent overvaluation. The 1967 devaluation should have come earlier. The 1981 recession which devastated British manufacturing was associated with a major overvaluation of the (floating) pound. In the EMS period of 1990–92 British export industry was once again the victim as it was in 1997–98.

It is also worth remembering that while one country may need to devalue, others will simultaneously benefit from their currency moving upwards. In 1992 the exit of the pound from the EMS was preceded by several newspaper reports to the effect that the Bundesbank was allowing it to be known that it favoured a devaluation of the pound. Whether or not this is true, and whether it was really in German interests for this to happen, it is safe to assume that the Bundesbank's interest in the matter was more that it was hoping to achieve an upward valuation of the Deutschemark to reduce inflation in Germany than a concern for the management of the British economy. But of course anything which would have prevented the pound devaluing would have prevented the desired rise in the value of the Deutschemark as well. EMU would have hurt both countries.

Although the evidence is clear that exchange-rate changes can be beneficial, it is easy to understand why many French policymakers have come to the conclusion that they lose nothing by giving up control of their exchange rate. This largely reflects their experience of the early 1980s, when their own inappropriate domestic policy did indeed generate a cycle of inflation and repeated devaluation. But there is no reason for the rest of Europe to be persuaded by arguments based on only an incomplete understanding of exchange-rate economics and a partial recall of history. Cost and price levels in one country occasionally rise above those in its trading partners. This might be avoidable in a perfect world, but we do not live in such a place. When it happens the appropriate combination of disinflationary domestic policy and devaluation restore equilibrium, and the ability to devalue or revalue is in this case an important tool.

What can be done in a monetary union?

The problems which lead to the need for a different policy might not occur. Policy references might not differ. Indeed, it is clear that most policymakers currently believe that the control of inflation should always be the overriding priority. However, this view is unlikely to persist forever, particularly if some countries seem to be doing much better out of the policy than others. It might also be hoped that responses to similar circumstances will also be similar, or at least will progressively become more similar if the euro exists for long enough. No doubt various proposals could be produced for speeding the process. Nevertheless, it needs to be appreciated that in so far as they are not the same at present, or that there are costs involved in making them more similar, these things are costs of the euro project.

When problems do arise a possibility is that changes in fiscal policy could soften the blow of harmful monetary policy. Where part of the monetary union is experiencing a boom and interest rates cannot rise because other countries are in recession, taxes might be increased to try to stop the boom. Thus in the case of Ireland joining the euro with its economy growing unsustainably quickly, a sufficient increase in taxation might, by cutting off the boom, prevent any great problem arising. The opposite case of a country in recession while the rest of the monetary union needs interest rates to rise is rather more difficult in the European case. In principle, taxes could be cut and government expenditure increased to combat the recession. However, the Maastricht Treaty and subsequent agreements place limits on the level of government borrowing, so this avenue is largely closed off. This is a particularly foolish aspect of the Treaty which will be considered at more length in Part 2 of this chapter.

This asymmetry is one of the reasons there is every danger of the euro being recession-prone. Booming countries can deal with this problem by raising taxes, but the ability of recession-bound countries to take the appropriate fiscal action is severely restricted. On average we must therefore expect a more significant problem with recession than boom.

An alternative would exist if the European Union had power to tax and spend sufficiently large amounts in each country. Then it could reduce the damage from a common monetary policy by taxing booming regions and spending the money in countries in recession. This is one of the things central governments do when different regions of one country experience different conditions; indeed, the effect arises largely automatically from the operation of the tax and benefit systems. In the EU the central budget is too small and too committed specifically to agriculture to operate in this way, although the possibility that this will change will be considered in Chapter 5.

Another theoretical possibility is that unemployed labour might migrate from one country to wherever there are jobs. The United States functions effectively as a monetary union, despite the fact that different areas have non-synchronous business cycles, largely because many people are willing to move across the country if necessary. There are obvious difficulties with this in the European Union because of language and other cultural barriers, so labour is much less mobile. Thus the alleviation of the problem through this route will be negligible.

Another difficult, although unaddressed, issue is that of the extent to which it will be politically acceptable for economic sacrifices to be required of one part of a monetary union in the interests of other parts. Even in the United States, there are resentments when one part of the country feels that interest rates are being raised because of inflationary pressures in other parts. But the United States is a well-established nation state. Along with these resentments there is also a deeper acceptance that this is the way policy must be set. The same largely applies in the United Kingdom. East Anglia may suffer from British policy, but people in East Anglia do not give the impression that they feel the way policy is determined lacks political legitimacy or infringes their rights.

But what of the south of Italy and Germany? Or Greece, should it ultimately join, and the industrial centre of Europe? What of Ireland, even, and the rest of Euroland? At some point circumstances will arise where lower interest rates are required in one of the poorer countries than are forthcoming from the central bankers in Frankfurt. Are we to suppose that the central policymaking apparatus of the European Union has sufficient political legitimacy for this to be acceptable in whichever country is suffering? In many ways, this may be the most dangerous aspect of the whole experiment.

It is for this reason that Christopher Huhne's Table 3.1 (page 37 of the reverse part of this book) and his arguments about correlation co-efficients among different European countries and different regions of the United States are beside the point. They aim to demonstrate that there is about the same tendency for economic performance to diverge among European regions as among parts of existing countries, so that, on the face of it, there is about the same need for separate policy. But a divergence between two European countries sharing the same currency is far more serious than a divergence within a culturally and politically more homogeneous area such as an established nation state, which is also operating a reasonable national fiscal policy.

So, as a theoretical possibility, it could be that the costs of having a common currency in Europe may never manifest themselves. However, even on the basis of the arguments in this section, the risks are great. In the worst case of a boom in one place and recession in the other, Euroland will face an unsolvable policy problem. Whatever action is taken, the results will fall well short of those that could be achieved with separate currencies. Since there are three clear cases of this circumstance already having arisen since the Treaty was signed, in the original 12 countries alone, it is hard to see how it can be confidently assumed there will never be another.

The economic case for the a single currency in Europe, then, is the case for risking a large amount for a small gain, with almost a certainty of losing.

PART 2 THE DANGERS OF THE MAASTRICHT PLAN

The Maastricht plan is, however, much more than just a plan for a common currency. It also contains a blueprint for how economic policy is to be conducted once the monetary union is formed. For this reason, the issues considered in the previous section are far from being the only ones of importance. The issue of monetary union cannot be treated simply as a matter of whether Europe would or would not be well served by a single currency.

The problem with the Maastricht Treaty is that it prohibits and prevents the implementation of good economic policy. It does this in various ways. First, by creating a central bank to run policy over which no other body is to have any influence, and by requiring it to give absolute priority to price stability irrespective of the consequences. Second, by imposing arbitrary and foolish rules limiting the ability of the governments of the member states to use policies of taxation and expenditure to pursue the other fundamental objectives of economic policy: employment and growth. Third, by pretending that good policy is simply a matter of making rules to be administered by technicians and that political accountability has no role in economic policy in democracies.

Although these rules threaten economic prosperity in Europe and indeed possibly the world, it does not follow that the objectives of the Treaty – low inflation and limited government indebtedness – are themselves undesirable. It is a question of how these objectives should be achieved, and how their achievement interacts with the achievement of other objectives. The presumptions behind the Maastricht Treaty are that, notwithstanding great evidence to the contrary, they are easily achieved, and that, again in contradiction of the facts, they automatically bring with them the achievement of all other goals. The truth is much closer to the opposite: rules like those of the Maastricht Treaty have been tried and they do not work. Such rules do not bring prosperity, they bring economic failure.

The theoretical presumptions of the Maastricht Treaty are that the central bank's policy has no significant effects on employment beyond short periods of time; that the European Union need concern itself only with its domestic objective of price stability and ignore issues of economic performance in the rest of the world; and that good fiscal policy is achieved by discipline and firmness rather than by a proper understanding of the relationship between the government's taxation and expenditure decisions and the behaviour of the private sector.

First, it is important to see what the Maastricht Treaty says. Next the rationale which is given for the provisions of the Treaty can be considered. Then it will be argued that the theoretical presumptions are wrong, and indeed that this has been demonstrated by recent European experience.

What the Treaty says

The Maastricht Treaty deals with much more than monetary union. It covers citizenship, consumer protection, the environment, policing and many other matters. But these things have all been agreed; there is no British opt-out from them. Only the issue of the British membership of EMU remains to be settled, and this is what is considered here.

The independence of the European Central Bank

It is clear that the adoption of a single currency means that there must be a single central bank, replacing the separate central banks such as the Bundesbank and the Bank of France and, potentially, the Bank of England. This single central bank will take over the function of controlling interest rates.

It has become fashionable in many countries to take the view that monetary policy is best carried out by a central bank which is 'independent'. However, independence means different things in different countries. In the United States, the Federal Reserve System is in certain respects independent of presidential and congressional control; but it is statutorily required to pursue a variety of objectives and in practice its obligation to report to Congress, and its desire to avoid prolonged conflicts with the administration, mean that it typically pursues a fairly balanced policy. In Britain, the Bank of England is responsible for setting interest rates to achieve an inflation target which is set by the government and can be changed by the government.

However, the Maastricht Treaty categorically rejects the view that there should be any democratic input into monetary decision-making at all. It is remarkably firm on this point. It even forbids governments to 'seek to influence' the central bank. Article 107 of the Treaty says:

> Neither the ECB nor a national central bank, nor any member of their decision-making bodies shall seek or take instructions from Community institutions or bodies, from any government of a Member State or from any other body. The Community institutions and bodies and the governments of the Member States undertake to respect this principle and not to seek to influence the members of the decision-making bodies of the ECB or of the national central banks.

So although other independent central banks are quite clearly under the control of elected governments in important ways, such as having their targets set for them by the government, or at least being ultimately subject to legislation, the European Central Bank (ECB) is to be protected by international treaty, even from attempts to influence it.

This is a remarkable departure for the European Union, which is an organisation supposedly committed to the principles of democracy, and it is surprising that the formulation of Article 107 has not attracted more attention. In Britain, together with the move towards independence, there has also been careful attention to the accountability of the Bank of England to the elected government and also to that government's right to set the objective of the central bank. Whether even this kind of independence is desirable is debatable, but it is certainly not the gross breach of democratic principles entailed by the Maastricht Treaty. Nor is the British case exceptional. Even in Germany there is no legal provision which goes as far as the Maastricht Treaty, and for most of its history the Bundesbank has in practice been highly sensitive to the desires of the government.

So the Treaty is no simple reflection of the fashion for central bank independence. It is a far more extreme and threatening version, and one which denies even the ultimate accountability of the central bank to the people. As we shall see, when combined with the objective which the central bank has been given and the difficulty of changing the Treaty, this independence is not just objectionable, but dangerous.

The objective of price stability

The ECB, besides being made independent, has been given an unchangeable objective, that of achieving price stability. Again the wording of the Maastricht Treaty is remarkably clear. Referring to the ESCB (the European System of Central Banks), meaning the ECB itself as well as all the national central banks, Article 105 of the Treaty says:

> The primary objective of the ESCB shall be to maintain price stability. Without prejudice to the objective of price stability, it shall support the general economic policies of the Community with a view to contributing to the achievement of the objectives of the Community.

It is a remarkable characteristic of this part of the Treaty that price stability is made the overriding objective. Other objectives are considered, but it is explicit and clear that they are secondary and may be pursued only when price stability is secure. Given a conflict between economic growth and price stability, or employment and price stability, or, indeed, any measure of prosperity and price stability, prosperity comes second and price stability first.

It is sometimes said in defence of the Treaty that the national governments maintain power over whether to join an exchange-rate system, and that this would in practice give them the power to control interest rates. If it is interest rates that control inflation, then they have, by the back door, a way to overrule the central bank. Whatever the theoretical merits of this view, it is immaterial since there is no prospect of there being an exchange-rate system for Europe to join. Another possibility, allowed for in Article 109, is that the national governments may formulate 'general orientations for exchange-rate policy'. This too might seem to give a route to influencing the exchange rate. However, the same article says that these orientations shall be 'without prejudice' to the primary objective 'to maintain price stability'. Once again, therefore, it is the central bank which is in control, and the goal of price stability which dominates.

A second remarkable aspect of Article 105 concerns the definition of the stated objective: price stability. Some of the countries which have recently made their central banks independent have also adopted this objective, but in those not involved in the Maastricht process the government retains the right to instruct the central bank as to what is meant by price stability. The Maastricht Treaty confers no such rights on other bodies. Consequently, it is difficult to take the expression to mean anything other than what it says, which is that the ECB must pursue a zero rate of inflation. The indications are that it will seek to achieve a measured inflation rate of 0–2%. Some advocates present this as a great concession, but it is no such thing. Measured inflation is understood to overstate actual inflation by around about 1% owing to the limitations of the way data are collected. Therefore, achieving a measured rate of 0–2% means an actual rate of between plus and minus 1%, or, on average, zero.

This is remarkable since no major country in western Europe has achieved this in the post-war period for more than a year or two at most, although for much of this time they have been aiming for something near it. Even in Germany inflation has run fairly consistently at moderate levels. Figure 3.1 shows the German rate of inflation in the period before the oil shocks (it has been higher since). In the supposedly golden age of price stability before the 1970s, in the supposedly most inflation-averse country, the Maastricht target was achieved in some years, but fewer than half. What is the chance of making this policy stick throughout the European Union today? Or, at least, what is the chance of making it stick without severe damage to prosperity?

THE ARGUMENTS AGAINST THE EURO

Figure 3.1   **German inflation before the oil shocks, 1951–72**

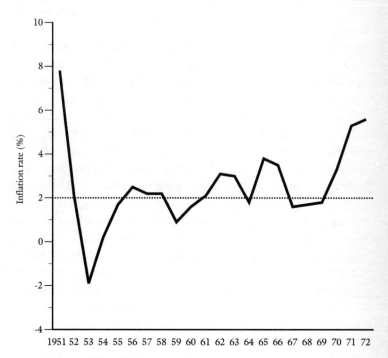

Source: IMF International Financial Statistics.

A more reasonable objective might be aim for 'low inflation', and it would have been easy to use these words in the Treaty if this was what was intended. But the Treaty says price stability, without qualification or limitation. As we shall see, the absolute prioritisation of price stability is, beyond any reasonable doubt, the road to economic disaster.

The Stability Pact
The Maastricht Treaty also restricts national fiscal policies. Article

104c 1 says simply, 'Member states shall avoid excessive deficits.' The fiscal deficit is the amount that a government borrows in a year, which is usually measured as a percentage of national income. More surprisingly, if member states fail to respect this requirement the European Union has the right, by Article 104c 11, 'to require the Member State concerned to make a non-interest-bearing deposit of an appropriate size with the Community until the excessive deficit has, in the view of the Council, been corrected' and 'to impose fines of an appropriate size'.

The details of the size of fines and circumstances in which they would be imposed were worked out in 1997. The rules are that, in principle, a country will be fined if it has a fiscal deficit of more than 3% of national income unless its national income fell by 2% or more in that year. Thus if there is a severe enough recession it will be excused the fine when it borrows too much. In other cases, whether the fine is actually imposed is subject to a vote, but first we should consider what the consequences of imposing the fines would be.

As a preliminary point, the concession that a 2% fall in output means there will be no fine is not nearly as generous as it might seem. In the 29 countries listed in the Organisation for Economic Co-operation and Development (OECD) *Economic Outlook*, which are broadly speaking the richest countries, in the period 1981–99 (including forecasts) there have been 13 cases of output falling by this amount or more. This means that out of a possible 551 data points, under 2.5% recorded such falls.[10] Of these, three were accounted for by the dramatic Scandinavian recession of the early 1990s and one by the British recession of 1991 (associated with ERM membership); six more were accounted for by Mexico, Iceland and Turkey. This leaves one each in the United States, Canada and New Zealand, but no others in Euroland. Evidently, if the concession is to be meaningful, it must be that the authors of the Maastricht Treaty fear that their policy framework will result in many more severe recessions than there have been in the recent past.

If any such fine is ever levied, it will be an extraordinary imposition on national sovereignty, without parallel anywhere in the world. The federal government of the United States, for example, does not impose rules on the budgetary policy of the states, and certainly not fines, although US states are usually thought to have rather less independence than EU member states. Some of the states have constitutional rules which bind them to balanced budgets, but this is a matter of an individual state's constitution, not a rule emanating from the federal government.

Before considering more fully why these provisions are so threatening to economic well-being, it is important to understand why they were adopted. Foolish as they are, they are not without a rationale in economic theory. And misleading though that rationale is, there are those who continue to find it in their interests to advance it as offering a proper understanding of the management of advanced economies.

Why does the Treaty say these things?

The natural-rate hypothesis

In 1968 Milton Friedman advanced the hypothesis that there exists a natural rate of unemployment. By this he meant, first, that left to itself the actual level of unemployment will remain around this rate, and, second, that the government cannot do anything, at least with monetary or fiscal policy, to keep the actual level of unemployment away from this level for long, although it might do harm in various ways if it tries. The basis of Friedman's argument was that labour markets work well in allowing people to sell their labour at the prevailing price if they wish to. If they do not wish to that is their business, but if they do, they will be able to. Unemployment, particularly long-term unemployment, is therefore more or less limited to people who do not wish to work.

It had been argued before Friedman, and was widely believed in the post-war period, that if the government were to undertake extra expenditure, financed by borrowing, this would increase the overall level of demand. The increase in demand would induce firms to hire more people, and this would reduce unemployment. Friedman's argument was that since this increase in demand does not originate in a change in individuals' preferences it lowers unemployment only by fooling them, and this can only be temporary. The government might, therefore, be able to engineer a temporary fall in unemployment, or a temporary rise, and booms and recessions might on occasion arise naturally. When in a boom, of course, unemployment would be below the natural rate, and when in a recession, above it, but these things would only be temporary.

There are other factors in this view which might affect unemployment on a long-term basis, but only by themselves being the determinants of the natural rate of unemployment. The most obvious of these is the level of unemployment benefit payments. If these are high enough more people will prefer to be unemployed, and therefore unemployment will be higher. Thus, argue the followers of Friedman, if a government wishes to reduce unemployment, lowering benefits and other similar measures will do some good. But as far as monetary policy and the overall level of government expenditure and taxation are concerned there can be no long-term effect on employment, either beneficial or harmful. Unemployment reverts to the natural rate.

Whether Friedman's argument for the existence of a natural rate of unemployment should really be considered part of the monetarist doctrine is a moot point, but it is not relevant. What is important is one inference that is routinely drawn from Friedman's argument: that monetary policymakers should give all their attention to the control of inflation and none to the control of unemployment. This is the idea that most clearly motivates the Maastricht Treaty.

There is no denying that Friedman's argument is a powerful one. But powerful or not, I shall argue that it is demonstrably false and that a disregard for employment in setting monetary and fiscal policy does great damage. First, however, we must note a further turn of the screw added to Friedman's hypothesis by later theorists, and the prevalence in modern thinking of the doctrine of policy credibility.

Two arguments for central bank independence

There is a peculiar aspect to the way the case for central bank independence has been made. Two quite different arguments have been advanced, in most cases without any clear distinction being drawn between them, even though they depend on more or less contradictory assumptions. As it happens both the arguments are false, but this does not stop them having a powerful influence on European policymaking.

The doctrine of policy credibility

The doctrine of policy credibility holds that an important determinant of economic success is the belief of businesses and individuals that the policymaker will maintain low inflation. The emphasis is definitely on belief in this argument. What the policymaker actually does is of secondary importance.

A typical formulation of the doctrine would be that if wage bargainers expect high inflation they will set high wage increases. This in itself more or less forces the policymaker to deliver high inflation; otherwise many workers will be priced out of their jobs by the high wages.[11] The resultant unemployment would be temporary, of course, according to Friedman's argument, but painful nonetheless. If the wage bargainers could be made to believe that there was going to be low inflation, they would agree lower wages and thereby make the low inflation possible. However, it is also said that once low wage increases have been agreed, the policymaker can achieve a temporary fall in unemployment by actually delivering high inflation. This awkward consideration is supposed to make it difficult to convince the wage bargainers, who are assumed to have a detailed understanding of the objectives of the policymaker, that inflation will be low, thereby leaving us permanently stuck with high wage increases and so, presumably, high inflation.

Sometimes the credibility argument is reformulated to say that it is not really the expectations of wage bargainers which are important, but rather those of financial markets. These markets, it is claimed, are permanently sceptical of governments because bursts of inflation have the effect of reducing the real value of government debt. Therefore a government wishing to reduce its debt without paying it back has an incentive to attempt to spring a surprise inflation on the markets. This, it is said, means the markets always demand higher interest than they would in the absence of this threat. As indicated in Chapter 2, the simple solution to this is for the government to issue index-linked debt.

The fashionable solution to the wage-setting problem is to assume that an independent central bank can undertake to deliver low inflation and the wage bargainers will believe this, whereupon the problem is solved. This idea makes it clear why the commitment of the Maastricht Treaty to price stability should be so uncompromising. Although it seems extreme, it is in fact rationalised by the doctrine of credibility.

Thus it is argued that central bank independence is a free lunch, in that it lowers expected inflation without any offsetting detriment. One or two charts purporting to support this view have been popularised by *The Economist* magazine, among others, in arguing for independence of the Bank of England. There are many problems with this evidence, but perhaps the most serious is that the analysis on which it was based has now been shown to be factually incorrect.[12]

'Politicians cannot be trusted'
Although the doctrine of credibility is fashionable among academic supporters of the euro, the more popular argument for central bank independence among both policymakers and commentators is that voters are myopic so that policy can be adjusted to secure short-term benefits before elections, even if this does long-term damage. Politicians, who are generally in the business of seeking re-election, are, in this argument, likely to lower interest rates before an election to reduce unemployment even if it means inflation rises after the election. The result is bad policy. In this case, the benefit of central bank independence is that the bankers have no electoral temptation and so policy is better.

Clearly, this argument depends on voters being short-sighted. If they properly understood what the government was doing, they would not be impressed and would presumably vote it out. This is rather in contrast to the assumption made in the first argument about the sophisticated insight into policy supposedly possessed by wage bargainers. Confusion is further heightened by the fact that the second argument is sometimes said to show that central bank independence improves credibility, even though the notion of credibility has no place in the account.

The idea of excessive deficits

In parallel to the theory of monetary policy which motivated the Maastricht Treaty, another theory claimed that fiscal policy can do no good either, but can do harm. It can do no good, it was said, because when governments borrow money they deprive some private agent of the funds, and thereby prevent a beneficial investment project being undertaken. It can do harm, it is claimed, in one of two ways.

The first argument is that when one country in a monetary union borrows, this has the effect of raising the interest rate that everyone must pay, including other governments. The one government's borrowing, allegedly, imposes a cost on other governments not of their making, and for this reason should be restricted. If this argument were correct it would have wide-ranging implications, since the same point could be made about any agent's purchase of any commodity. If one government purchases 'too many' paper clips no doubt their price will rise, but this does not make a case for legislation to prevent it.

A different argument, which is given much more prominence by the European Commission, is that if a government borrows too much it may eventually find itself unable to repay its loans. In such a circumstance, it is unlikely that a developed-world government would formally repudiate its debt, since this would have so many serious ramifications throughout the financial sector. In order to prevent this, however, a rescue might have to be organised by other countries. In the case of the European Union it is reasonable to suppose that much of the burden of such a rescue would fall on other members. The repayment of one country's debt would then fall ultimately on the tax-payers of other countries. This is what led Emerson *et al.* to claim that, 'Fiscal discipline defined as the avoidance of an unsustainable build-up of public debt is therefore a vital condition for the success of EMU.'[13]

There is no doubt, of course, that a default would be a serious matter. It is not clear why the fear of one should have become so prominent in the Maastricht process, since there would have been much the same consequences of default at an earlier stage. Be that as it may, the important issue is whether the danger of default is sufficient for it to be a major policy concern for the European Union as a whole, and, if so, what measures are likely to generate good, sustainable fiscal policy.

The errors in the Treaty
There is no such thing as a natural rate of unemployment
There is no doubt that Friedman's idea of a natural rate of unemployment has great appeal, and for many economists it has become the basic rule of thumb in thinking about unemployment. However, we should not allow theory to blind us to the facts, or be unduly impressed by the notoriously changeable fashions of economists.

There are two alternatives to the natural-rate view. One is the view that Friedman was specifically attacking: that unemployment can be permanently lowered by a policy of permanently higher inflation and that a government can in principle achieve any desired unemployment rate if it is prepared to put up with the corresponding level of inflation. This is sometimes known as the Phillips-curve view. Friedman's attack on this was certainly effective. But the trap lies in thinking that because the view Friedman attacked was wrong, his view must be right.

There is an alternative to Friedman's view which is much more important than the Phillips-curve view. This is the idea that the rate of unemployment which is currently achievable depends on the recent history of unemployment. So, for example, one consequence of a long

Figure 3.2   **British unemployment, 1975–96**

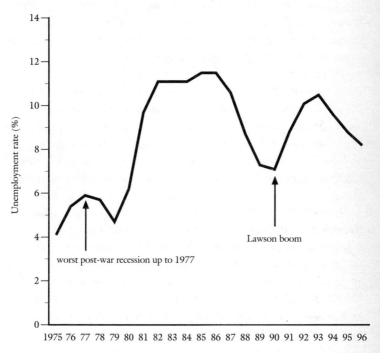

Source: OECD.

and deep recession, which temporarily raises unemployment above any estimate of its natural rate, is that for a long period thereafter it will be all but impossible to return unemployment to the levels previously attainable. This will be true whatever the level of inflation.

This idea, sometimes known as the 'hysteresis' view, is illustrated clearly by the British experience, shown in Figure 3.2. Between 1945 and 1979 the highest level of unemployment reached was 6% in 1977. At the time, such a level was thought to be a disaster. The Conservative government elected in 1979 advocated the natural-rate view, asserting that monetary policy could permanently change only the rate of inflation and that it could not affect unemployment beyond the short run. During the recession that followed unemployment increased well beyond 6%. It was claimed, however, that this would be temporary, and that once inflation had fallen, unemployment would return to its natural rate.

The sequel is now notorious. Unemployment did fall, but it was allowed to fall 'too far', so that inflation once again became a problem. A boom, now usually known as the Lawson boom, developed rapidly at the end of the 1980s and a further recession followed as the government once again tried to reduce inflation. Much argument has naturally taken place as to why the boom was allowed to go so far without corrective action and how the subsequent recession could have been ended. Much less often discussed is what happened to unemployment in this period. The lowest level that unemployment reached was 7%; that is, 1% higher than its level at the previous worst in the post-war period.

Since 1977 was a recession year, by Friedman's account unemployment (at 6%) must have been above the natural rate; and since 1990 was a boom year, unemployment (at 7%) must have been below it. Furthermore, 1977 was at that time the worst recession in the post-war period, and the boom of 1990 became notorious for its extravagance, so in each case the deviations from the natural rate should have been large. Clearly, the data contradict the view that there is any such thing as a natural rate of unemployment and show that long and deep recessions can have long-term effects on employment.

The natural-rate theorists have a response to this, which is to say that the natural rate may change depending on the incentives and organisation of the labour market. This gives rise to so-called supply-side policies aimed at lowering the natural rate. Policies usually claimed to improve the functioning of the labour market include lowering benefits and reducing tax rates, both of which are intended to encourage people to seek work. Reducing the power of trade unions and limiting workers' rights are also commonly mentioned. Other policies said to improve incentives might also be included, such as privatisations.

These supply-side policies are said, among other things, to lead to greater labour-market flexibility, and such flexibility is often said to explain why unemployment is lower in United States than in Europe. There is likely to be an element of truth in this, but it would be interesting to know how many of the economists who make this claim, or, indeed, how many readers of this book, are aware that the value of the jobseeker's allowance for a 24-year-old in Britain in 1998 was £39.85 per week or about £5.70 per day. This might be expected to engender a fair degree of labour-market flexibility since it is difficult to imagine that there are many voluntarily unemployed people contentedly living on such an amount. But that those who are unemployed for any length of time are voluntarily so is what the natural-rate hypothesis holds. This was the point of Friedman's argument.

However, the comparison of Britain and United States is not the important point, which is to compare Britain in 1990 or later with Britain in 1977 or earlier. During this time the supply-side conditions can only have improved. Marginal tax rates and the real value of benefits were cut, and union powers and workers' rights were reduced. These are the areas where the United States is said to be better than Europe. Yet, after the long, deep recession of the early 1980s, or slightly later in most of continental Europe, unemployment failed to return to the levels which were previously thought disasters, let alone to those which were normal. Therefore, whatever good the supply-side reforms did, it was not adequate to counteract the harm done by the disregard for unemployment as an objective of monetary policy during the period. This disregard led to a recession which did great and long-lasting damage in the form of a more or less permanently higher level of unemployment.

Nor is the British case exceptional. Among European countries the British experience, as regards unemployment, has been rather better than most. The case of France, shown in Figure 3.3 on the next page,

tries have not experienced the long and deep recessions that Britain and France have. So the US case is equally consistent with either the natural-rate view or the hysteresis view. Since so many European experiences resemble the British and French in contradicting the natural-rate view, we are forced to conclude that, elegant as Friedman's argument is, it is not correct. The labour market is a more complex market than his view suggests, and we cannot rely on quickly reaching a point where all who wish to work are able to.

The important consideration is that long and deep recessions, which leave large numbers of people unemployed, raise the minimum level of unemployment achievable thereafter. It is difficult to be precise about the reasons for this, although there are many possibilities. One is that many people unemployed for long periods of time lose their skills or motivation, or may appear to have done so, and are therefore less attractive to potential employers. Firms which are liquidated during the recession do not automatically come back into existence when the recession ends, so there is a permanent loss of the capital they scrap and of the firm-specific expertise of their former employees. Also, if recession is associated with an overvaluation of the currency, as has generally been the case in Britain, export markets are lost and not necessarily regained when the exchange rate falls again.

The consequence is that economic policy must not be set in accordance with the design of the Maastricht Treaty. Inflation is not welcome, but it does not follow that under all circumstances the achievement of price stability should be the exclusive goal of policy. Circumstances have arisen, and will arise again, where some mild degree of inflation is a far lesser evil than the long-term damage done by a deep recession which may be needed to eliminate all trace of it.

A good example of such circumstances is to be found once again in German unification. German policy was clearly unsuitable for the other EU member states, and they followed it to their cost. But there is another issue: was it even good policy for Germany? Unification brought many problems. Once it became possible for east Germans to buy western products they did so in fairly large numbers, and this led to a degree of inflation pressure. At the same time, once it became possible for east Germans to migrate to west Germany, they could not be expected to work in the east for substantially lower wages than were available in the west, so eastern wages rose. This, combined with economic collapse in the rest of eastern Europe and the former Soviet Union, did great damage to the profitability of east German firms, many of which went bankrupt, creating unemployment in the east. The German government decided against substantial tax increases to finance social security, investment subsidies and other payments that it was making to the east. It was forced to borrow the required amount instead, so there was a deterioration of German public finances.

Of all these problems, the Bundesbank decided that inflation was the one that should be tackled. It therefore increased interest rates. The consequences were a slowdown of economic activity, which increased unemployment in both east and west; an appreciation of the Deutschemark, which was particularly pernicious for the east German firms on the margin of viability; and, as a result of the deterioration in economic performance, a further deterioration of government finances. Almost ten years later the adverse consequences are still apparent. Unemployment remains at excessive levels, and Germany came within a whisker of failing the Maastricht fiscal criteria for EMU membership.

Although the best policy response to unification would have involved tax increases in the west, this was not within the power of the Bundesbank. It had to determine what interest rate to set, and there was an alternative to what it did: to accept a degree of inflation. Meanwhile, attention could have been given to the lack of competitiveness of east German firms and every effort made to keep in business those which might be viable by, most importantly, resisting a rise in the value of the Deutschemark, indeed, by seeking to lower it if possible.

This would have resulted in higher prices. It would also have moderated the rise in unemployment and the deterioration of public finances. It is a matter of judgment which is the more serious. But it is easy to see that the public debt which Germany has needlessly acquired brings a permanent cost; and unemployment has certainly not proved a temporary problem. German inflation, as it turned out, never rose much above 5%, hardly a level that would have been a catastrophe even if it had been somewhat higher.

Advocates of the euro like to argue that the reform of the east German economy would inevitably impose serious costs, so that the experience of the German economy since unification is wholly unrepresentative of anything which is to be expected in the future, but they should not be allowed to. The sustained increase in unemployment that Germany has experienced contradicts the natural-rate hypothesis on which the Bundesbank based, and the ECB will base, its policy, but there is nothing exceptional in this. The British and French experiences, as well as those of many other countries, also contradict it. It is true that taxes should have been raised in west Germany, but this does not excuse further bad policy by the central bank. In any case, the commitment not to raise taxes was made in the context of forecasts about the consequences of unification, which were much more optimistic. They said, in effect, that a great investment opportunity had arisen in east Germany, and that this would accelerate growth and therefore brought no need for increased taxes. These forecasts were based on the same favourable assumptions about the effectiveness of the free-market economy as the natural-rate hypothesis itself, and they also turned out to be badly wrong.

So the view that the control of inflation should always be the overriding priority has been tested in Germany, and it has been shown to lead to bad policy. Germany, as well as the rest of Europe, would have been better served by a policy that sought to balance economic objectives, not to prioritise one and only one above the rest. The German economy may have been successful for decades, but the policy of the Bundesbank, which is the policy of the Maastricht Treaty, has changed that.

The danger of the Maastricht Treaty, then, lies in disregarding unemployment and other objectives when seeking to control inflation. This certainly does not mean that inflation is beneficial, but it does mean that its elimination should not always be the sole objective. In particular, faced with inflationary developments over which policy-makers have no control, it should not generally be their priority to eliminate it immediately. In contrast, the Maastricht Treaty's insistence that the ECB achieve price stability seems to give no scope for anything else, whatever the cost in unemployment. This will be a tragedy, since it was the attitude in Britain in 1981, or Germany in 1990, or France for most of the 1980s and 1990s, and we already know that the costs are severe and long term.

Credibility is of no significance
The academic version of the credibility argument

Perhaps the most important challenge to the idea that credibility is all important in affecting the wage-bargaining process is that it is difficult to find instances of people bargaining their wages on the basis of what they think inflation will be in the future. Many people no doubt start off by thinking what wage increase is required to compensate for past inflation; a few perhaps project past inflation forward as a rough guide to what future inflation may be. But what the theory requires is that people form an acute sense of what the policymakers' incentives are under a variety of circumstances, and base their wage bargain on an assessment of how future policy will affect inflation. As a description of the world, this is plainly fantastic.

Second, there is the awkward point that all central banks now seem to think that policy takes two years to affect inflation, and the vast majority of wage bargains are for a shorter period. This means that at the time the wage bargain is struck, policymakers have no control over inflation for the period of the bargain. Therefore no issues arise about what the policymaker says future policy will be. What is happening is that policymakers take their decisions and then wage bargainers bargain their wages. If it is important to them what policymakers have done, they can find out. No issue about believing or disbelieving what they say arises.[14]

The argument that politicians cannot be trusted

This argument, although again fashionable, does not stand up to much scrutiny. The argument is that politicians are persistently tempted to adopt inflationary policy in order to win elections. But does inflationary policy win elections? If it is necessary to indulge in simple-minded explanations of electoral outcomes, a rather better picture comes from thinking of governments as being rewarded for doing what they say they will do.

The Heath government, in 1970, promised a free market and sound finance. It delivered nationalisation and inflation, losing power in 1974. Labour, elected in high hopes of peaceful relations with the trade union movement, was never more damaged than by the so-called 'winter of discontent' in 1978/79. Margaret Thatcher, however, is a clear case of a politician who did what she said she would do, although it was unpleasant, and was rewarded with election victory in 1983 despite unemployment rising towards 3 million. John Major survived the election of 1992 in most unpleasant economic circumstances promising commitment to the EMS; after the devaluation later that year his opinion-poll rating never recovered, and the government was defeated, although economic performance had been improving substantially ever since the devaluation.

The Lawson boom of the late 1980s appears to many people to offer a strong case for the political-manipulation view of economic management. Even if there were nothing to the contrary to be said, one example hardly establishes a general tendency. In fact, there is reason to believe that this boom was a genuine mistake. The lack of substantial independent commentary to the effect that policy was misdirected before the 1987 election, the failure to reverse policy after it, indeed the continuation of expansionary measures, and the fact that, fast though the economy was growing, this was broadly the outcome that had been promised as the reward for the policies of the early 1980s all point to its being a mistake; albeit, arguably, a foolish one.

It has also been widely, though groundlessly, asserted that the public disputes between the then chancellor of the exchequer, Kenneth Clarke, and the governor of the Bank of England, Eddie George, before the 1997 election demonstrate the case for independence. At that time interest rates were controlled by the chancellor. The governor persistently advocated an increase on the basis that he felt that in two years' time inflation would be too high. The chancellor made a different judgment and refused the increase, earning plenty of criticism from the financial press for political manipulation and such like, and some more from Chris Huhne. Yet two years later it can hardly be said there has been a major inflation. If it takes two years for monetary policy to affect inflation, as is widely agreed, and the quality of monetary policy is to be judged by the inflation rate it delivers, Kenneth Clarke's decisions have been entirely vindicated. An interest-rate increase in early 1997 would have been wrong and damaging. We were lucky not to have an independent central bank at that time and on these terms there is no case to answer that there was a political manipulation taking place.

Lastly, as regards the most important points of economics, there is the issue of whether interest-rate changes are a sensible way for politicians to try to buy votes anyway. Many savers are hurt by interest-rate cuts, and this factor must counteract the borrowers who benefit. There is also the point that tax cuts offer an alternative to interest-rate cuts. Most voters pay tax, so most votes would, on the assumptions being made, be for sale. If the problem is that elected people, rather than doing broadly what they perceive to be in the national interest, are merely in the business of buying votes, it makes no sense to focus on central bank independence as the remedy.

Probably more important than the logical deficiencies of this argument is the attitude we are invited to take to democratic accountability. It is an assumption of the Maastricht approach that unelected, unremovable and unaccountable individuals will pursue the general interest. Personally, I am much happier with the view that people who fail, or who pursue sectional or personal interests, can be fired. Democratic accountability is not usually thought to be a threat to good and fair policy, but its guarantor. The fact that the opposite view is now becoming engrained in the thinking of the European Union is one of the more frightening aspects of recent developments there.

Balancing the government budget can be damaging
What is good fiscal policy?
There is no doubt that a default by a government would be a serious matter. Equally, there should be no doubt that there is much more to sound fiscal policy than the reduction of deficits; and, indeed, even the avoidance of default, or the danger of it, may not be an entirely simple matter of reducing government spending or increasing taxes. The Maastricht rules certainly have the effect of preventing the proper use of fiscal policy, and the countries that have been seeking to follow them have not achieved satisfactory fiscal positions either.

The truth about fiscal policy is that governments of developed countries routinely run deficits. No serious problem need arise, as it would for a household, because developed economies continually grow, so that the government's tax base is always increasing. It is surprising at first sight, but nevertheless quite clear, that a government can borrow every year and still have a stable or even falling burden of debt relative to national income. British government debt today, even if calculated at constant prices, is far in excess of what would have been sustainable in the 19th century. But so what? British national income is far higher too, and so the debt can be sustained.

Beyond this, a proper understanding of fiscal policy needs to see government borrowing in the context of the behaviour of the private sector and the activity of the economy as a whole. The crucial point is that economic transactions are two sided. If the government spends less money, someone receives less. If instead of spending less the government taxes more, it is much the same: someone else has less.

Whoever has less will also presumably spend less, which is the same thing as another person receiving less. All the people receiving less will then pay less in tax, so the government's revenues will fall. Consequently, the government's borrowing will not fall by as much as its spending since the cut in spending itself causes a fall in tax receipts. This means that the achievement of a balanced budget, or a nearly balanced budget, is much more complex than it seems. It is emphatically not a matter merely of hard decisions on spending cuts or tax increases, and the presumption that it is neglects the economic effects of these actions.

It is sometimes argued that a government which is trying to balance its budget can cut expenditure and counteract the tendency of this to lower employment by reducing interest rates. This is supposed to encourage the private sector to invest more, thereby generating jobs and hence tax revenue. But in the context of central bank independence, and certainly monetary union, the interest rate is controlled by someone else. We are more likely to find ourselves in the position of having monetary policy causing unemployment and fiscal policy being prevented, by the Maastricht rules, from acting as an antidote. In any case it is far from clear that interest-rate reductions automatically call forth extra investment of just the required amount.

It is true, of course, that overall saving and investment will be equal, but it is a mistake to think that saving by the government therefore automatically increases investment by the private sector. When the government saves more (or borrows less), the private sector as a whole suffers a fall in its income because it is receiving less money from the government. This fall should be expected primarily to cause private-sector saving to decrease, not investment to increase. The reasons are that at a lower level of income the private sector has less money to save, and, at the same time, investment projects will, if anything, be less attractive because the private sector also has less money to spend. So sure enough, saving and investment are equal, even after the government saves more, but it is because income has fallen enough to decrease private saving rather than because investment has spontaneously increased in response to government cuts. The odd 0.25% cut in interest rates is unlikely to counteract this, and in adverse conditions there may be no interest rate low enough to call forth sufficient extra investment to maintain employment in the face of government expenditure cuts. In Japan, for example, interest rates have been cut more or less to zero without ever having the desired effect on investment.

If conditions become bad enough, private agents may think it in their interests to save more as a precautionary move. Any extra saving is just like the government reducing its borrowing in implying a fall in others' income. It will make investment projects less attractive too.

Therefore the view that balancing the government budget, or moving from a larger to a smaller deficit, necessarily improves overall economic performance depends on one of two mistakes. Either it is being forgotten that an action by the government which reduces its expenditure or raises its income necessarily also reduces the income of the private sector as a whole. Or it is being assumed that private-sector investment depends only on the interest rate and not at all on the general degree of economic health, and in particular private-sector spending power, and that some unspecified, but convenient, force causes just the right degree of investment to be called forth by any government tax or expenditure change.

A good demonstration of the problems of fiscal management again comes from recent European experience. Once the European recession after German unification began to be felt, causing government revenue to fall and expenditure to rise, several governments began to fear that they would fail to meet the convergence rules, and in particular that their fiscal deficits would be above 3% of national income. The case of France is illustrative. In 1993 its fiscal deficit was 4.5%.[15] The OECD reported that 'the 1994 budget aimed at unprecedented expenditure restriction'. The next year, after this restriction, the French deficit was 4.8% of national income. In its 1995 annual report on France the OECD reported that 'the 1995 budget ... aimed at expenditure restraint and a further fall in the deficit'. This time the outcome was a deficit of

4.3% of national income. In 1997 the OECD reported 'the 1996 budget was again aimed at expenditure restraint and a further decrease in the deficit', and in 1996 the deficit was 3.9% of national income. Thus unprecedented restraint followed by years of further contraction had only a marginal impact on the overall budgetary position. In the end, as is well known, France and several other countries were only able to achieve a deficit of below 3% by what became known as fiscal fudges, meaning creative accounting. All their determined economic policy, which imposed so much hardship through expenditure cuts and so much long-term damage through government investment cuts, failed to bring the forecast results.

It is important to be clear that this sequence of policy decisions was motivated by the same theoretical outlook as is now encapsulated in the Stability Pact. Although these events took place before 1999, the convergence criteria to which governments were trying to conform are similar to the Stability Pact rules. Nor can it be pretended that this failure is owing to German unification. That took place in 1990. It cannot explain the failure of expenditure cutting to bring a significant fall in the French government's deficit five years later. Although it would be convenient to advocates of the Maastricht plan to argue it, there should also be no question that the failure of policy was owing to a lack of will on the part of the government. The OECD reports make it quite clear that the hard choices were being made. The problem was that the economic theory on which the policy was based is inadequate. What happened was that French expenditure cuts damaged the French economy, and that prevented the government's finances improving.

So what should we do? It is no easy matter to construct appropriate rules for fiscal policy. This fact itself speaks against the simple rules of the Maastricht programme. However, it is certainly asking too much of governments to offset every change in private-sector behaviour. For this reason alone economic fluctuations are inevitable.

The danger of the Stability Pact is that it prevents the exercise of sensible judgment and pushes in the direction of counterproductive policy. Faced with an economic downturn, a government finds its finances worsening. If it is in danger of breaching pact limits, it must start to raise taxes and cut expenditure, both of which worsen the downturn. If the downturn becomes bad enough the fiscal rules are relaxed, but by then the damage has been done. Good, or even reasonable, fiscal policy would avoid output falling by 2% in a year. For the Maastricht rules to bind governments to bad policy unless this happens is obviously foolish.

Can we hope that the fines will not be imposed? Yes, this is always a possibility. However, there are two serious reasons to doubt that this will be an effective remedy. First, the doctrine of credibility argues that rules must be strictly imposed. What will the financial markets think if the first time the pact is breached, political leaders of the European Union club together and vote not to impose a fine? This consideration alone suggests that the fine will be imposed in order to preserve the EU's 'credibility'.

Second, even in the absence of a fine, we should still expect countries to be shy of breaching the agreed limits and then having to be dispensed from the fine. Since, furthermore, fiscal control is far from being an exact science, governments will presumably wish to be well clear of the limits. This consideration points towards a permanent and general attempt at fiscal contraction to provide security against either being fined, or being embarrassed by being let off the fine.

This creates a significant danger of generally contractionary policy. It is all very well for Christopher Huhne to suppose that governments will have to aim at something like a balanced budget in order to be safe from the fine. But this is not good policy. First, there is no powerful reason to seek a balanced budget on its own merits. Developed-country incomes grow and therefore a growing public debt associated with a normally unbalanced budget can be sustainable. Second, it is not clear that the achievement of a balanced budget on average will be reasonably practicable. The French, and others, found it difficult if not impossible to achieve a deficit of under 3% in time for the euro in

1999, despite having seven years to achieve it since they signed the Treaty. Why should it be so easy to achieve a balance any time it is desired without causing unemployment?

What we need is not a collection of international fines on governments that borrow too much, but a recognition that the government's borrowing is to a large extent determined by the decisions of the private sector, and therefore that healthy public finances are to a great degree the outcome of a healthy economy. Imposing discipline on public finances is much more likely to worsen private-sector confidence and lower investment than it is to promote the investment which, if it occurred, would automatically result in an improvement of the public finances. Treating the symptoms, in this case, makes the disease worse. We should be looking at what makes an economy healthy and expecting the achievement of this to improve public finances, rather than expecting cutting government expenditure somehow to improve the health of the economy.

It is worth noting that in opposite circumstances even balancing the government budget may not be sufficient. If private-sector spending is sufficiently high the government should be in surplus. In this case, even a balanced budget leads to excessive demand. It is easy to imagine a government spending too much in a boom through being unduly impressed that its budget was balanced. The signs, on the basis of the theory behind Maastricht, would be that the government was doing a good job, exercising prudence and promoting stability by balancing its budget. But there is no reason to suppose that good management should not require a considerable surplus. Indeed, it is surely part of the explanation of the Lawson boom that the chancellor was persuaded that since the government finances were healthy nothing else could be wrong, but this turned out to be a great mistake. This consideration lies behind the idea that the government budget should balance over the trade cycle, meaning that it will be in surplus during booms and in deficit during recessions. This is all very well, but there is no automatic mechanism to ensure that the degree of surplus or deficit will be the right one. In any case, neither the Maastricht rules nor the Stability Pact place limits on budgetary positions over the trade cycle. They simply place limits on deficits.

The problem of international co-ordination

A further ramification arises from the international effects of budgetary policy. If small countries have a strict balanced-budget policy it may not hurt them. Fluctuations in demand at home can be offset by changes in exports, roughly maintaining employment. Thus the fact that Luxembourg and Switzerland have had long histories of economic success but have rarely borrowed more than tiny amounts is no surprise. Even Germany in the period of its greatest success borrowed little and exported much, but the significance of Germany in the world economy was much less then than now. No doubt this also explains why so many US states choose to have balanced-budget policies. Each state is small, so individually their budgets are of little significance.

However, a large economy, say the whole of the European Union, cannot expect to escape in this way. A fall in demand in the EU is not likely to be offset by an increase in exports, since such an increase would have to be huge relative to the rest of the world's total imports. Indeed, the problem will be made worse if a recession in Europe also reduces imports from the rest of the world, as presumably it must. This will push the rest of the world's economies in the direction of recession as well, presumably reducing European exports to them.

It is easy to see how this attitude can lead to global economic disaster. If we suppose that the collapse of South-east Asian economies can be corrected only by an increase in their exports, which seems a natural assumption, this means that the rest of the world, including Europe, must import more. The US economy has grown fast for several years, but it is unlikely that a rapid growth of imports can be sustained much longer without either inflation or the balance of payments becoming a serious problem. This suggests that Europe must import more. For Europe to import more, Europeans must spend more, or produce less.

The latter outcome would mean that unemployment would rise in Europe from its already high level. Alternatively, if Europeans are to spend more, this extra expenditure must come from either the government or the private sector. If the private sector wishes neither to reduce its saving nor to increase its investment, only an increase in government expenditure can lead to the required increase in imports. This is a matter of logic, not theory. But if the Maastricht rules prevent the government from increasing its expenditure there is no way out. South-east Asia stays in recession. In due course European exports fall and the danger of a worldwide recession grows.

What the world as a whole desperately needs, then, is a European policy which acknowledges the international interdependence of the economies. The idea, which has been emanating from the ECB, that Europeans should look after their own problems and leave the rest of the world to sort themselves out, is a denial of this basic fact. Yet the notion that other countries should put their own houses in order simply makes no sense when it is recognised that economic transactions are two sided. We cannot have a policy of Asia exporting more without a policy of someone else importing more. For this to happen, without an increase in unemployment, someone must spend more.

The fiscal consequences of Maastricht

Although any country can find itself in difficulty because of excessive government budget cutting, three considerations make the problem worse in the Maastricht case. First, the rules are incorporated in an international agreement and are therefore much harder to change than the rules of thumb governments adopt for their own purposes. The details of the rules are not part of the Treaty itself so they are easier to change than the central bank statutes. But they are still embedded in international agreement.

Second, they are associated with fines. With a proper understanding of fiscal policy these are a strikingly bad idea. The fines would have to be levied on just those governments in no position to pay them. We are to contemplate the case of a government which has been unable to cut its deficit, although it will presumably have made some effort to do so, thereby bringing about a recession. It is then required to raise taxes to pay the fine. The authors of this proposal seem to think that excessive borrowing by a government is analogous to a road-traffic offence and that a firm enough punishment will deter future infringements. But we are dealing with governments whose every financial action affects the balance of the economy. In the case envisaged, the extra 'discipline' or 'commitment' expected of the delinquent government can lead only to action which further reduces private-sector incomes and hence worsens recession. It is incomprehensible that anyone could imagine this to be the way to build a successful political union.

Third, the fiscal rules are being imposed just when the ECB's monetary policy will be coming into effect. The monetary policy is in danger of creating recessionary circumstances all too often, but it is absolutely inevitable that it will do so somewhere at some time. In these circumstances rendering fiscal policy impotent as well creates a serious problem and then makes it unsolvable.

Might defaults happen?

The Maastricht rules are foolish rules because they force governments into counterproductive policy. But this does not mean that a government default would not be a serious matter. The fact that as long as governments conduct normally prudent policy there should be no danger of a default does not, unfortunately, mean that when policy is set in accordance with the Maastricht presumptions, such a danger can be ruled out. Table 3.1 on the next page shows the change in the ratio of government debt to national income between 1991 and 1996, expressed as a percentage.

Out of 15 countries, all of which broadly adopted the Maastricht outlook on policy priorities and most of which were committed to meeting fiscal rules to qualify for monetary union, only one, Ireland, the beneficiary of a high level of foreign investment, managed a signi-

Table 3.1 Ratio of government debt to national income in
EU member states, 1991 and 1996 (%)

	1991	1996
Austria	58.1	69.5
Belgium	127.7	126.9
Denmark	62.3	66.7
Finland	23.0	58.0
France	35.8	55.4
Germany	41.5	60.4
Greece	92.3	112.6
Ireland	95.3	72.7
Italy	101.5	123.8
Luxembourg	4.2	6.6
Netherlands	78.8	76.6
Portugal	68.7	68.1
Spain	45.8	70.6
Sweden	53.0	77.4
United Kingdom	35.5	54.2

Source: OECD (1998).

ficant reduction in its debt ratio, and three managed small improvements. The performance of France and Germany, the two leaders of the process and principle authors of the Treaty, is truly spectacular. In 1991 a Treaty was signed which was to exclude from EMU any country with a debt ratio greater than 60%. No doubt France and Germany, starting from ratios of 36% and 42%, felt they had written a Treaty that made their own membership safe. Yet within five years there was a serious question as to whether they would be able to meet the criterion. Once again it should be emphasised that these have not been years of profligacy by European governments; they are not years of vote-buying politicians ruining the public finances to secure re-election. No, they are years of the Maastricht policy in action; years of central bank independence, sound money and prudence. They are years of the things that we are promised in a monetary union will secure our well-being. Had the Maastricht rules been more tightly interpreted, countries with debt ratios well over 60% would have been excluded. This proved to be too much of a political embarrassment, so the rule was for practical purposes ignored. But now it may be necessary to face some unpleasant consequences of that decision.

It having been demonstrated that the Maastricht approach does not result in falling government debt ratios, it is an unfortunate fact that the issue of the ultimate solvency of some countries may come into question. Having started from high levels of debt some countries have been unable to reduce it. Indeed, in most the level of debt has grown. It cannot be imagined that debt as a proportion of income can grow forever without insolvency resulting, but then we have to wonder what is going to reverse the process in the worst-placed countries, Italy and Belgium.

It is said that what will make all the difference is that once EMU is under way interest rates will fall, and this will allow governments to repay debt since their interest charges will be lower. But there are two considerations counting against this view. First, if the circumstances in which Europe now finds itself are that there is more likelihood of an Italian default than a German one, the interest rates these governments pay will not equalise. Who would lend to the Italian government for the same return as they can have from lending to the German government? And if the Italians must still pay more interest, their ability to reduce their debt is compromised.

Second, the politics in the most debt-ridden countries is such that it will not necessarily be possible to maintain the low expenditure and high taxation that has been in place in recent years. The Italian government, for instance, trading on the popularity of the European project in Italy, has introduced one major tax specifically to allow Italy to qualify for the euro. But when that specific promise is made, what guarantee can there be that it will be possible for governments to maintain such a tax once membership has been secured? If they cannot, and if there is no substantial economic recovery, the issue of the ultimate solvency of these governments may quickly come into question. If it does so, the interest rate they must pay on their existing debt will rise, driving them to either more borrowing, increasing the total debt, or more taxation, limiting the amount of economic growth they can expect. Either way, it becomes hard to see a rapid improvement in their debt ratios. A further recession, perhaps originating in Asia, or an interest-rate increase in response to inflationary pressure in another part of Euroland could quickly spell disaster.

4 Is Britain special?

It is frequently argued that the British economy is different from those of continental Europe in a fairly permanent way and that this changes the balance of advantages and disadvantages of the euro.

One argument is that British trade patterns have traditionally been less European in their orientation that those of other countries. Consequently, we have less to gain from the removal of transactions costs and exchange-rate uncertainty within Europe and more to lose from any increased exchange-rate uncertainty with respect to the rest of the world.

The second argument is that more people in Britain have variable-rate mortgages than in most of Europe. British consumers are therefore more sensitive to interest-rate changes than those of, say, Germany. Therefore a European Central Bank (ECB) seeking, unavoidably, to employ a one-size-fits-all interest-rate policy to manage the whole European economy will, other things being equal, impose much more violent swings on Britain than elsewhere. It is also true, although the point is less frequently made, that British companies have rather more variable-rate loans than their continental counterparts. Again, therefore, we are better off preserving our own interest-rate policy.

The idea advanced by Chris Huhne – that the higher proportion of flexible-rate loans is offset by a higher proportion of flexible-rate assets – is only half right. This characteristic does go some way to limit the difference between Britain and other countries in their overall responsiveness to interest-rate changes, but there is still the issue of the severity of effect on individuals. In the event of steeply rising interest rates, for example, many British households could find themselves unable to pay their mortgages. The fact that other British people would at the same time be benefiting, which is the extent of Huhne's point, would not be much consolation. In a hypothetical case where this situation is extreme enough to lead to large numbers of defaults in Britain, the solvency of British financial services firms would be in danger, not those of other European countries.

The third frequently heard argument is that Britain is an oil producer and that changes in the price of oil therefore affect Britain differently from other countries. In so far as such a change calls for different policy in oil producers from that in oil consumers, it argues against being locked into the same policy. Again the argument is correct. A change in the price of oil is the most obvious although far from the only example of an asymmetric shock.

On the other side of the coin, special characteristics of Britain are sometimes alleged to make the euro more desirable there than elsewhere. The role of the City of London in financial services is said to give Britain much more to gain by being intimately involved with monetary developments. This seems to have much less going for it than the other points. It is difficult to see that effects on one sector of the economy should determine national policy in such an important area. But in any case there is no strong reason to think that London will be disadvantaged in the provision of financial services to Euroland by being located outside it. Financial services is the most globalised industry in the world, largely because it has almost zero transport costs. If this were not true it is difficult to see how Switzerland or for that matter the Cayman Islands, both outside the European Union since it began, could be the successes they are.

Should we follow the herd?

It is sometimes said that since most members of the European Union are joining EMU it is in British interests to join, notwithstanding the fact that we would rather the plan had never been devised. Of course, if the euro is economically damaging to Europe, we should wish that it had never been adopted. Britain will certainly suffer if there is an economic disaster in continental Europe. Recession there will damage our exporters and to some degree communicate a recession to Britain, and indeed the world. But it does not follow from this that conditions will be worse outside the euro than inside. Outside, at least we have some opportunity to insulate ourselves by pursuing more balanced economic policies, and policies more appropriate to whatever position we find ourselves in. It is nonsense to argue that a great mistake has been made in continental Europe and that therefore it is in our interests to make the same mistake.

Most of the European Union is committed to the Maastricht plan, and if the merits of the proposal are not substantially different for Britain, there is a paradox in arguing that Britain should remain outside. The temptation is to assume that an assessment of the euro's economic merits has been made in continental Europe, that a favourable outcome has resulted in its enthusiastic adoption, and that a marginally different assessment has led, temporarily at least, to its rejection in Britain. The truth is quite different. The alleged economic benefits are not the driving force anywhere in Europe. It is everywhere a matter of political commitment buttressed by some convenient arguments in economics.

Two things are quite different in Britain. The first is that we have been much more inclined to debate the issue on its economic merits. The strong presumption in many minds is that if it is a good idea we should join, and if it is a bad one we should stay outside. The economic arguments, once they are properly considered, indicate that the Maastricht plan, if not the whole idea of a single currency, is a bad idea, and in the worst cases a catastrophic one.

The second difference is that the political project is more popular in the rest of Europe than in Britain. This has resulted in approval for EMU which would not have been forthcoming if the economics had been more closely considered. In this connection the Euroenthusiasts should note that absolutely the most they can hope for is Britain joining the euro with a great many people opposing this policy. The

Euroenthusiasts must recognise that it is not only the divisions in the Conservative Party which have forestalled a British commitment to the euro; there is a great division in the country as well. There is no possibility in the foreseeable future of the British people in general becoming enthusiastic for the euro. This means that when the euro begins to impose costs, even if the enthusiasts were right in their happy assumption that these would be outweighed by benefits, there is likely to be more resentment of this in Britain than elsewhere. In the wider scheme of things, this will damage the objectives of the Euroenthusiasts. Instead of supposing that they can induce good feelings about Europe by imposing common institutions, it would be much better strategy for them to accept that they must first build the legitimacy of the existing institutions in the hope that this engenders support for further steps. Britain is special in this regard simply because British people do, on the whole, feel rather differently about integration than most of the others. This should quite properly affect policy.

Will we lose foreign investment if we remain outside?

An argument along the same general lines – that the euro might be undesirable but if it is going ahead we should join – is that remaining outside will result in a loss of foreign investment. A few high-profile companies have said that they will reduce investment in Britain in these circumstances. However, some have welcomed the possibility of Britain being outside, correctly observing that we are inside the common market and this gives free trade access to the whole of the European Union, whether part of the euro or not.

One thing which we should expect to have a significant impact on foreign direct investment is the general economic success of the country. From this point of view remaining outside is far preferable to joining. If the European economy suffers the kind of deflation that the Treaty seems to require, it will not be a happy place for investors. Britain will look far more attractive.

THE ARGUMENTS AGAINST THE EURO

Will we be punished for remaining outside?

An argument which appears slightly more powerful at first sight is that Britain will become subject to reprisals from the rest of Europe designed, in the manner of economic sanctions, to force entry to the euro. It is difficult to know what the motive for these sanctions is supposed to be, and rather easier to see reasons for Euroland to refrain from such action.

A good example concerns the TARGET system for financial settlements. Various European leaders asserted that the City of London would be excluded because Britain was not to be in the euro, and Euroenthusiast doom-mongers were quick to take up the call. No doubt they all felt a propaganda coup had been scored. In reality, a few months later a perfectly satisfactory agreement was reached giving London access to it.

A slightly different version of the argument holds that a consequence of the monetary policy in Euroland will be to cause the value of the euro to rise in international exchanges, thereby harming the competitiveness of Euroland's exporters. Britain and other countries outside would be the beneficiaries of this in the sense that their firms would become more competitive, while European free trade would continue to guarantee free access to continental markets. Sometimes this is called a competitive devaluation by Britain and other outsiders. The unfairness, it is said, of gaining market share because of exchange-rate movements would warrant retaliation, perhaps in the form of tariffs.

The first difficulty with the argument is that it is an attempt on the part of advocates of the euro to have their cake and eat it. The basis on which it is said that EMU is desirable is that exchange-rate changes bring little in the way of benefits. This is why we are encouraged to give up separate currencies. But then, apparently, we are also to believe that exchange-rate changes are powerful enough to warrant retaliatory sanctions. Equally, the basis on which the Maastricht plan is advocated is that the single-minded anti-inflationary policy of the ECB will result in economic prosperity. But, again, this same policy will bring the exchange-rate developments which are to do such harm. If Britain is to have an advantage from being outside that could possibly warrant sanctions, this surely must show the whole project is undesirable. If advocates of the euro are not willing to take that view, they must give up the sanctions story.

What of countries which are not members of the European common market? They will presumably be gaining similar advantages. Are they to be subject to trade sanctions as well? Perhaps it is felt that outside the common market their access to European markets is in any case highly restricted, so Euroland has not much to fear. To have this made explicit would be interesting, since the European Union presents itself as a friend of free trade in the world, whereas this outlook clearly implies that it is protectionist with respect to non-members.

Another question arises. Are the Euroenthusiasts really telling us that our continental partners are engaged in running a protection racket worthy of any Chicago mobster of a few decades ago? We must join the union, they say, or pay the price in exclusion from the free trade area in Europe. Apart from such an exclusion breaching the Treaty of Rome and numerous world trade agreements, and constituting a revocation of the British opt-out to which our partners freely agreed, it would be an extraordinary way to seek an ever closer union.

I find it hard to hold the European Union in such contempt as to suppose that such sanctions would develop. It is strange that those who profess themselves enthralled by the European ideal are the ones who believe that this is the way Europe operates. If they do, what lies ahead? Are we to be told in future that we are forced to sign up to every European proposal on pain of economic sanctions? Where will the process end? If this were true, then surely we should consider a compete withdrawal from the European Union and its nasty predatory practices.

Fortunately, it is not true. Britain has negotiated an opt-out, and our partners consented to it when they signed the Maastricht Treaty.

The advocates of Europe cannot be serious in suggesting that our closest partners and allies will revoke the Treaty piecemeal as it suits them, nor that we should wish to be even closer partners and allies if they do.

5 Can the Treaty be improved?

Will it be all right on the night?

When confronted with the undesirability of the Maastricht rules, an increasingly frequent response of advocates of the euro is to argue that there is nothing to worry about because once EMU is under way, the rules will either be ignored or changed. The European Union, they say, is a pragmatic organisation and the commitment to making the euro work is great, so things will be sorted out. In other words, it will be all right on the night.

This is a peculiar argument for advocates of European integration to use. It involves disowning the Treaty they advocate and admitting that it is a bad Treaty, and implies that we should presume our European partners incapable of making a biding agreement. Thus it is said the Treaty is only a scrap of paper and not a basis for policy.

More important than its peculiarity, however, is the fact that this is a risky argument. Several considerations suggest we should not rely on good sense prevailing. There has been little sign to date of any such attitude. The details of the Stability Pact were agreed only in 1997, well after the folly of the Maastricht rules had been exposed. By then it was apparent that government expenditure cuts were inhibiting recovery in their own countries as well as those of their neighbours, but that did not stop a 'stability' pact requiring fines being agreed.

The culture of price stability at all costs is deeply ingrained in the Bundesbank and is sure to be inherited by the European Central Bank (ECB), which is so closely modelled on it. Indeed, for a long time, it was highly successful in West Germany. The fact that it has had unfortunate results since German unification should be a double warning: first, that the Maastricht policy is a bad policy; and second, that the policy will nevertheless be followed. No one forced such a damaging policy on the Bundesbank, but it adopted it, the French followed suit and so did most of the European Union. What is supposed to be different once EMU has begun?

Still worse than the facts that the lessons have not been learned, and that arguments for a different policy framework do not command general assent, is that there are powerful vested interests supporting the Maastricht framework. Central banks should not be expected to give up their independence easily, and they will constitute a powerful lobby to preserve the Maastricht framework. Many businesses, rightly or wrongly, perceive themselves as beneficiaries of a low inflation policy. In Germany the terms of the Treaty are widely seen as safeguarding low inflation against the desires of other countries to pursue a different policy. To change the objectives or remove the independence of the ECB requires the unanimous agreement of all the signatories of the Treaty. There is no prospect of this. Indeed, it is difficult to imagine many governments making such a proposal because it would inevitably appear to be an attempt actually to raise inflation. The rules are foolish rules, but it is not so easy to propose their amendment, however balanced and sensible a policy a government wishes to pursue, without seeming to advocate irresponsibility.

There have been a few rumblings from some of the governments embarking on EMU to the effect that the rules of the Stability Pact should be relaxed, but little comfort should be taken from this. In the first place, it can hardly be said that the mild relaxations being proposed represent a reassessment of the role of fiscal policy in economic management, which is what is required. It has also become apparent that the ECB and others who see themselves as custodians of the 'wisdom' of Maastricht are determined to resist these moves as strongly as possible. The great problem with the Treaty is, of course, as with central bank independence, that it puts European law very much on their side.

There is also an internal logic of the Maastricht framework which argues against even contemplating changes in the Treaty. This is where the doctrine of credibility is so important. When people are in the frame of mind of thinking that only binding commitments can bring the all-important private-sector expectations into the desired position, revoking these commitments appears certain to damage economic outcomes. The alleged danger of losing credibility is bound to be invoked if any proposal for relaxing the Maastricht rules gains even the mildest support among European governments.

Lastly, there is room for significant doubt as to whether the European Union really is so pragmatic and able to change bad rules as advocates of the euro, and integration more generally, assume. One example will suffice. The Common Agricultural Policy, 38 years after it was created, continues to raise food prices, distort markets, wreak environmental havoc, dominate the EU budget, damage the standing of Europe in the eyes of the rest of the world, endanger world trading arrangements and provoke continual discord between the members of the Union. When is this going to change? Can we afford 38 years of the Maastricht rules?

A European fiscal policy

A different kind of change in the Treaty has been suggested: the creation of a European fiscal policy. The argument is that EMU will indeed create unemployment in some countries. This could be remedied to a degree with fiscal policy in these countries, except that the Stability Pact makes this difficult, if not impossible. The solution therefore is a federal fiscal policy, which will also have the effect of taxing richer countries and transferring the money to poorer countries. This may go some way towards moderating differences in business cycles.

From a certain perspective this proposal clearly has merit, independently of the discussion of EMU, although it is difficult to see how it could be welcomed by anyone opposed to political union. It would necessitate granting powers to an EU institution either directly to tax citizens or to assess taxes on member governments and leave it to them to raise the money and hand it over. Equally, of course, it is difficult to see that such a development can be envisaged by those supporters of EMU who continue to deny that it is a significant step towards political union. It cannot logically be believed that monetary union involves no significant steps towards political union, and that to be successful monetary union needs a federal fiscal policy, and also that monetary union will in fact be successful. Yet this appears to be the position of some advocates of the euro.

Others, however, have started to describe the creation of a European fiscal policy as inevitable, and from the perspective of making EMU a success it would certainly be an improvement on the policy framework contained in the Maastricht Treaty. But it is not clear that it will be acceptable. Germans will understand that they are being asked to pay, and others will expect to receive, but such a Treaty amendment would require unanimity. In the event of Britain joining the euro, what do we suppose will be the attitude of the British government? We can hardly expect an opt-out from a device which is alleged to be essential to the success of the euro, but we would expect on average to be contributors to, rather than recipients from, such a device.

From the point of view of the management of the European economy, a federal fiscal policy is certainly better than what we are offered. But if advocates of the euro wish to stand by the claim that the European Union is pragmatic, and problems are solved as they develop, they should face the fact that the improvement required in the Treaty is not the addition of more supranational power, but the scrapping of the policy framework and its replacement by a balanced attitude to the objectives of economic policy and the methods of pursuing them. This is simply not on the horizon. If it ever comes about, we should reconsider British participation. But at present the European economies have been blighted by the same attitude as is enshrined in the Treaty, and we should give no credence whatsoever to the hope that all will mysteriously change once the euro is under way.

6 The political consequences of the euro

Is the euro intended to promote political union?

Undoubtedly, those who have been most energetic in advancing the euro see the project as leading to political union. Why else would Jacques Santer, president of the European Commission, have described the finalising of the original membership of the euro as 'a landmark date on which European integration took on a new momentum'?[16] Indeed, it is difficult to find continental politicians who express any doubt about this presumption, although in Britain many, even among advocates of political union, have been reluctant to see the euro as promoting further steps along that road. Nevertheless, this is exactly what the Treaty of Rome calls for. The stated goal of European integration is 'ever closer union'. British politicians, and occasionally continental ones, advancing particular steps have found it in their interests to deny that each step is part of a larger project, but it is.

There may be a few, predominantly in Britain, who imagine that EMU can be implemented and that will be the end of the story, but this defies sense and the history of the European Union. A good example is the way EMU itself was advanced. The previous major step of integration, variously known as the single European market, the internal market programme or just '1992', had been agreed by Britain and the others with no commitment to monetary union or other further steps of comparable importance. Much of the advocacy of 1992 centred on estimates of economic gains popularised for the European Commission by Michael Emerson and others.[17] Before the programme was even scheduled to be complete, Euroenthusiasts were advocating EMU on the basis that a single market needs a single currency, a consideration which had been notably absent from the discussion of the benefits of the single market. Again a document was produced by the Commission estimating economic benefits. Many of its arguments flatly contradicted ones that had been advanced in the earlier book, but no matter, the earlier one had served its purpose.[18] The British government had a legal right to veto the EMU plan but did not do so. The other countries reacted to the possibility of a veto by creating the device of an opt-out: the rest would go ahead, but Britain would be allowed to remain outside.

The next move in the game, which is the stage we have now reached, is for the Euroenthusiasts to assert, first, that since the euro is going ahead, we are more or less forced to join; and second, that no important further steps are entailed, and if any are suggested Britain will have a legal right to veto them.

It is further argued that Britain's standing in the European Union can be improved by our joining the euro. Apparently, by this act we will cease to be seen as the awkward partner and become a more respected and influential member of the Union. But once Britain joins there will be other controversial proposals, and the Euroenthusiasts should face the fact that there will be opposition to them. Indeed, some are already being made, apparently on the assumption of a quick British entry to the euro. *The Times* of November 18th 1998 reported on an agreement which apparently seeks to promote 'a culture of regulation' and tax harmonisation, among other things. If the British people are prepared wholeheartedly to adopt these things, then so be it, but if not, then joining the euro will certainly not change Britain's reputation as the awkward partner.

As usual, these new proposals are accompanied by the claim that tax harmonisation is made necessary by preceding agreements, in this case the introduction of the euro. But if so, why was the cost of harmonising taxes not previously admitted as a cost of the euro? What other discoveries of 'necessary' accompaniments are about to follow? It will not be long before we are also being told that we can sign up to whatever proposals are currently on the table because nothing further is entailed, and if anything is suggested we will have a veto. But the lessons of history are clear enough and we should know what to expect by now.

Why supporters of political union should reject the euro

The fact that monetary union is a step towards political union is not in itself a reason to oppose it, since there are those who genuinely favour political union. For them to oppose the euro is much harder, but the truth must be that a monetary union which is economically damaging will retard, if not destroy, the integration process.

The danger to the European project arises from the fact that recessions, and economic distress in general, are rarely conducive to internationalism. Although a perfectly respectable case could be made that times of economic failure are the times when most is to be gained from openness and trade, to imagine that these things are ever in practice likely to follow from economic failure is foolish.

It would be remarkable if anyone were to claim that the successes achieved by neo-Nazi parties in several European countries, most noticeably in France, are unrelated to the economic failure of recent years. Of course unemployment at persistently high levels has bred racism in France. The outlook of these groups is one which the vast majority of British supporters of the euro would find objectionable, but why has their support grown so much as the Maastricht Treaty recession has developed? Why has neo-Nazism returned to the German political stage? Why have extremist movements enjoyed such success in so many countries?

Once the euro is introduced the problem will become worse. First, an undesirable policy being imposed from a foreign city, with the national government having no control, since it no longer controls the policy instrument, will be politically provocative. It should be remembered that it is inevitable that policy interests among countries will differ at some point in the future. The estimates of the costs of this have wholly disregarded the issue of political resentment building up. Yet it is impossible to imagine unemployment rising in a poorer member of Euroland because richer members are suffering mild inflation without such resentments. Equally, it is hard to imagine inflation rising in Germany without corresponding resentments. These resentments will count against the idea of Europe. They will be aggravated, moreover by the unaccountability and lack of legitimacy of the European institutions which will be imposing the policy.

Second, whatever ill effects the Maastricht plan has on European businesses, it should be a great opportunity for political entrepreneurship. We cannot expect adverse economic developments imposed from foreign cities by unelected bankers not to lead to the creation of political movements specifically to oppose these things. Such movements will probably hold politically objectionable views along with their economically more sensible ones. A general disapproval of European integration and internationalism is likely, accompanied by a tendency to blame foreigners and racial minorities for economic failure. These political movements, which are already evident in many countries, will prosper in the policy environment of the Maastricht Treaty. They are also likely to profit from the attitude taken in so much advocacy of Maastricht, that democracy is in any case a flawed form of government and that we are better off handing over our basic economic interests to bankers and other appointed experts to do as they please.

It is not necessary to go as far as Professor Martin Feldstein, who suggested that the threat of war between west European countries could be revived.[19] The danger, in its mildest form, is merely that the standing of the integration project will be damaged by the perception that national economic distress is being imposed by outsiders. In a slightly worse version, there will be pressure for trade protectionism to safeguard jobs. Thus could European free trade lose the legitimacy it has progressively gained. In such circumstances, there is no doubt that some political group will find it in its interests to advocate withdrawal from the euro, and perhaps from the European Union. If the economic conditions are bad enough this position will prove attractive, whatever its theoretical limitation. In any case, it is difficult to imagine that the

European Union as a whole will not be pushed in a protectionist direction by such developments, threatening the world trading system.[20]

The likelihood of these developments does not depend on the introduction of the euro being disadvantageous overall. I have argued that it will be damaging and recessionary for the whole of Europe and for the world at large, and this will certainly make matters worse. But whatever happens there will be losers somewhere at some points. It is in those places at those times that the fabric of European integration, and perhaps European democracy, will begin to unravel. The basic reason is that the political process will not support damaging policy imposed from a different country by unaccountable bankers. The political process in existing countries permits much more, but European integration has not reached the point where this is possible across the continent.

The right way to develop the European Union is to build the institutions on the foundation of their legitimacy in the public mind. To await, therefore, the genuine feeling of the peoples of Europe that their interests are sufficiently interlocked such that it is appropriate to have one economic policy for the whole continent. The hope that imposing a single policy will engender its own legitimacy contradicts common sense, and furthermore takes a huge gamble, not just with our economic fortunes but with our political institutions as well.

Thus the right course for those who earnestly hope for a United States of Europe is to oppose monetary union at present. At the very least they must oppose it until a policy framework is agreed which balances many interests in economic policymaking, rather than presuming even the slightest inflation to be not merely the greatest but the only evil. On these terms, whether a role could be found for EMU as a means of enhancing the legitimacy of the European Union might become a debatable issue. At present, under the Maastricht framework, such fragile legitimacy as Europe enjoys can only be lost in monetary disaster.

7 Conclusion

Monetary union has been the dream of the Euroenthusiasts, in Britain as elsewhere, since the outset. At last at Maastricht in 1991 it seemed the dream was fulfilled. There was a commitment by 11 countries to a specific timetable leading to a common currency. This plan is now being implemented, and many in Britain fear that our standing in Europe will again be damaged by delay in joining.

It is true that much that the European Union has done has been good for Britain, as it has for other countries. In many respects it could have been better if British foreign policy had been more alert and we had participated more eagerly in the good European schemes at an earlier stage. But it makes no sense to join a monetary union now because we regret not joining a customs union in 1958.

Despite the benefits of Europe there have been, and the greater ones there could have been, the Euroenthusiasts need to rethink. The estimated benefits of the euro, small as they are, have probably been exaggerated, and the economic costs of monetary union have been much understated. Everything points towards the desirability of different policies in different countries. Even in the United States, a much more closely integrated economic area than the European Union, different regions experience different conditions. There have, as I have reiterated, been three clear cases in the 1990s of different policy being required in one country from that required in the majority of the European Union. These circumstances are not rare events, associated with oil shocks and little else; they are a permanent, recurring feature of developed economies.

To some extent the need for different policies is mitigated by labour mobility. This does much to account for the success of the United

States. But Europe is far from having the same degree of labour mobility as the United States and will progressively move further from it as more countries join the European Union, introducing more linguistic and cultural diversity. So we cannot expect European monetary union closely to resemble that of the United States.

Of course, it is only monetary policy that must be the same throughout a monetary union. To some extent appropriate fiscal policy can compensate for the damage done by inappropriately unified monetary policy. It can never fully compensate, but it can mitigate. This is also probably part of the story of US success, but again things are not the same in Europe. There is no federal fiscal policy. National fiscal policy might do the job, but is constrained by the very agreement creating the monetary union. So again Europe faces the problem of differential developments without having the means to deal with them.

There is more. The Maastricht rules create a permanent and unqualified prioritisation of the control of inflation and place policy in the hands of central bankers, who are by intention less accountable than any central banker, or probably any public servant of any kind, has ever been in a democracy. This is no accident. It is a deliberate response to the doctrine of policy credibility. Revocable commitments can be revoked, therefore only irrevocable ones are persuasive. Thus the statutes of the European Central Bank can be changed only by the unanimous agreement of every national parliament, and in some cases national referenda as well.

In general, the Euroenthusiasts respond that it will be all right on the night. Never mind that the Treaty is a bad Treaty, Europe is still a sensible environment for achieving good policy. There is nothing to fear. But is this true? What about the Common Agricultural Policy and the Common Fisheries Policy? When will this sensible organisation resolve these issues? Why did the British budgetary dispute take so long to resolve in the 1980s? Why has there been such a failure of the European Union to assert itself in foreign and security affairs, even within the European continent?

THE ARGUMENTS AGAINST THE EURO

More strikingly, why was the Treaty written this way in the first place if it is agreed to be so foolish? I wonder how many of the Euroenthusiasts are among those who are proud of not having read the Maastricht Treaty. But for any who have read it, there are some extremely lucid parts and most of them relate to the importance of central bank independence, the absolute prioritisation of price stability, the restriction of fiscal policy and the exclusion of elected representatives of the people from the policymaking process. All the things, in other words, which the complacent advocates say we should suppose it does not mean.

Since the Treaty was agreed, unemployment rates all over the continent have been stuck at levels unprecedented since the Great Depression. Why? Because of world recession, perhaps? No. The United States has been booming for most of the period, as was most of Southeast Asia until recently. Because of the burden of supporting East Germany? But could a state a fraction of the size of west Germany have dragged the whole of the largest economic area in the world into a decade-long recession? Hardly. The cause of the great European recession of the 1990s has been that independent central banks, obsessed by their 'credibility', and budget-cutting governments have been implementing the Maastricht policy rules since the Treaty was signed. Interest rates have been too high, the Deutschemark and all the currencies tied to it have been overvalued and government expenditure has been inappropriately cut. Europe has suffered the Maastricht Recession.

So let no one say that the Maastricht policy framework is a good one. Even if Europe was, late in 1998, at last recovering, the evidence is clear: the Maastricht policy framework is a bad one. But let no one say either that the framework is a bad one but there is nothing to worry about, since it will not be followed. It has been followed. Disaster or not, we can see clearly the danger that the policy will be followed since it has been for so long. The minimum condition of British participation in EMU should be that it be established on sound principles of economic management and democratic accountability. There really need be no further discussion until this is achieved.

But there is more to worry about. European institutions lack legitimacy. These institutions are to have direct control of some of the most fundamental determinants of economic well-being for most of the continent. And they have an impossible task. It is inconceivable that the same policy will suit all parts of Euroland all the time. Even if policy is not in future a deflationary disaster for the whole continent as it has been recently, it is sure to be deflationary for some parts at some times. As Chris Huhne says, the area stretches from Helsinki to Cadiz and Sligo to Brindisi. Somewhere, sometime, there will be recession while the rest of Euroland booms. Then interest rates will rise for the whole area and the country or region in recession will suffer.

Some consideration of the political consequences of this circumstance is now urgent. There will be deep resentment and it will be a resentment for which there is no useful outlet. Not protest to the national government, which has given up its powers; not protest to the real economic government in Frankfurt, since even if it were inclined to recognise an objective other than price stability, it can do nothing for one region in recession while others boom.

These dilemmas already arise in our existing countries, but we have three essential antidotes. We have some degree of labour mobility and reasonable fiscal redistribution. These things are not always enough, but they do help. We also have deeply rooted feelings of the identity of the nation states. This makes it acceptable, in most cases, that there is one policy for the whole country. There are a few exceptions to this. Separatist movements exist in parts of several European countries, and this is surely a most persuasive argument that the European Union cannot expect to escape such movements when policy starts to damage some part to the benefit of others. It is widely questioned in Scotland whether Scottish economic interests have been served by government from London. How can it be doubted that the same question will be asked about government from Frankfurt by whoever suffers from its policy?

THE ARGUMENTS AGAINST THE EURO

I fear, too, that the political movements arising from these circumstances will not all be in most things moderate. High, persistent unemployment breeds racism, not just separatism. And it is objectionable organisations which will benefit from the Maastricht policy. No doubt they will also benefit from the fact that so many people have now followed the Bundesbank's lead in denying the role of democratic accountability in economic governance. It may then, if generally adverse circumstances develop or divergences between different country's interests become too great, not be inappropriate to doubt the hold of liberal democracy on the European political process. This is the greatest fear of all.

So Europe is in a mess. Should it turn back, having come so far, and look foolish, or go on, accepting the consequences? In the best case the consequences are mild. Some transactions costs are saved and fortune favours the project with a world environment conducive to painless price stability and a European one without too many serious divergences of interest. It should be obvious to turn back, because in any circumstances less favourable than these a heavy economic price is paid. The dreamers continue to dream that the economic price can be paid and somehow the European Union will become ever more popular, but it can only be a dream, not reality.

But turning back seems impossible. The ghost of the Werner plan haunts the project, too many important individuals staked too much on it, and it has to be carried out. In Britain we are luckier. We are not committed and in every way we are entitled to remain outside the euro. This will not allow us to avoid all damage, but with sensible, balanced policy, it will allow us to avoid much of it. Nor is it Euroscepticism which should keep us out. Eurosceptics have no difficulty in knowing that they wish to remain outside the euro. That is quite logical. But it is the Euroenthusiasts who should fear Maastricht the most; the Euroenthusiasts who should regret that it has come so far; and, above all, the Euroenthusiasts who should be most determined in opposing British participation in a bad European project.

Notes

1 Gros and Thygesen (1991).
2 The expressions 'interest rates in Germany' or 'German interest rates' mean the interest rates that apply to Deutschemarks, not the rate that applies to any money which happens to be in Germany. It is possible to open a dollar account in London and the interest rate will vary more or less with American rates, not British ones; it is an 'American interest rate'.
3 Emerson *et al.* (1992).
4 Emerson *et al.* (1992), especially pages 75–77. They emphasise, for example, the benefits that would come from more European involvement in environmental policy, the desirability of a 'free internal energy market in electricity' and several other things with no connection to monetary union.
5 Emerson *et al.* (1992), pages 66–8.
6 Emerson *et al.* (1988), page 79.
7 Emerson *et al.* (1992), page 73, 'the empirical research has not found any robust relationship between exchange-rate variability and trade'. Today the situation seems to be much the same.
8 Emerson *et al.* (1992), pages 83–84. When these opinions are not favourable, as for example over the minimum wage or indeed the Social Chapter more generally, strangely little is heard about them from this source.
9 Emerson *et al.* (1992), page 138.
10 OECD (1998).
11 Another formulation of basically the same idea was discussed earlier. In that case the focus was on what agents expect the exchange-rate policy of the policymaker to be, but much the same

line of thinking applies.

12 By, I am embarrassed to report, Forder (1998a).

13 Emerson *et al.* (1992), page 107.

14 There are many other theoretical errors in supposing that the credibility problem, if there is one, can be solved by central bank independence, and I confess to having gone into them in some detail in Forder (1998b).

15 All the fiscal deficit numbers for this discussion come from OECD (1988). The comments on French budgetary policy come from OECD (1994), (1995) and (1997). These are the OECD's reports on policy and economic developments in France.

16 European Commission (1998).

17 Emerson *et al.* (1988).

18 The major contradictions are highlighted by Peter Oppenheimer and his co-author (1996).

19 Feldstein (1997).

20 A possibility I have explored more fully in Forder (1998c).

References

Alberola, E. and Tyrvainen, T. (1998) 'Is there scope for inflation differentials in EMU? An empirical evaluation of the Balassa-Samuelson model in EMU countries', Discussion Papers, 15, Economics Department, Bank of Finland.

Andersen Consulting (1998) *Business, Britain and Europe: the first 25 years*, European Movement, London.

Arrowsmith, J. (1998, July) 'Large scale EMU: the May council decisions and implications for monetary policy', *National Institute Economic Review*, London.

Arrowsmith, J. (ed.) (1998) 'Thinking the unthinkable about EMU: coping with turbulence between 1998 and 2002', National Institute Occasional Paper No. 51, London.

Arrowsmith, J., Barrell, R. and Taylor, C. (1998, October) 'Managing the Euro in a Tri-polar World', paper presented at the 21st colloquium of the Société Universitaire Européene de Recherches Financières, Frankfurt (mimeo).

Balassa, B. (1964, December) 'The Purchasing Power Parity doctrine: a reappraisal', *Journal of Political Economy*.

Baldwin, R. (1989, October) 'The growth effects of 1992', *Economic Policy*.

Baldwin, R. (1990) 'On the microeconomics of EMU', in Commission of the European Communities, *One Market, One Money*.

Bayoumi, T. (1989, August), 'Saving Investment correlations: immobile capital, government policy or endogenous behaviour?', IMF Working Paper No. 89/66.

Bayoumi, T. and Masson, P.R. (1996) 'Fiscal flows in the United

States and Canada: Lessons for monetary union in Europe', *European Economic Review*.

Brandner, P., Diepalek, L. and Schuberth, H. (1998) 'Structural budget deficits and sustainability of fiscal positions in the European Union', Working Paper No. 26, Oesterreichische NationalBank, Vienna.

Bureau Européen des Unions de Consommateurs (BEUC) (April, 1988) *Transferts de l'Argent a l'intérieur de la CEE*.

Canzoneri, M., Diba, B. and Eudey, G. (1996, June) 'Trends in European productivity and real exchange rates: implications for the Maastricht convergence criteria and for inflation targets after EMU', Centre for Economic Policy Research, Discussion Paper No. 1417.

Centre for Economics and Business Research for the Confederation of British Industry (1992) *The impact of UK attitudes to the EU on inward investment into the UK*.

Centre for Economics and Business Research for the Corporation of London (1998) *The City's Importance to the European Union Economy*.

Commission of the European Communities (1977, April) *Report of the Study Group on the role of Public Finance in European Integration* (The MacDougall report), Brussels.

Currie, D. (1997) *The pros and cons of EMU*, Economist Intelligence Unit, London.

Davidson, I. (1998) *Jobs and the Rhineland Model*, Federal Trust.

Deutsch, R. (1998, January) *The advent of a true euro corporate and high yield market*, Merrill Lynch.

Dornbusch, R., Favero, C. and Giavazzi, F. (1998, April) 'Immediate challenges for the European Central Bank', *Economic Policy*, No. 26.

Eichengreen, B. (1996, December) 'EMU: an outsider's perspective', Center for International and Development Economics Research (CIDER), Working Paper No. C96-079, University of California, Berkeley.

Eichengreen, B. and Wyplosz, C. (1998, April) 'The Stability Pact: more than a minor nuisance?', *Economic Policy*.

Emerson, M. and Huhne, C. (1991) *The Ecu report*, London.

Emerson, M., Aujean, M., Catinat, M., Goybet P. and Jacquemin A. (1988) *The Economics of 1992*, OUP, Oxford.

Emerson, M., Gros, C., Italianer A., Pisani-Ferry J. and Reichenbach H. (1992) *One Market, One Money*, OUP, Oxford.

Engel, C. and Rogers, J.H. (1996, December) 'How wide is the border?', *American Economic Review*.

European Commission (1990, October) 'One Market, One Money', *European Economy*, No. 44, Luxembourg.

European Commission (1998) *Infeuro Newsletter*, No. 8.

Fatas, A. (1998, April) 'Does EMU need a fiscal federation?', INSEAD Working Paper, *Economic Policy*, No. 26.

Fatas, A. (1997, January) 'EMU countries or regions? Lessons from the EMS experience', *European Economic Review*, Vol. 41.

Feldstein, M. (1977) *Foreign Affairs,* Vol. 76, No. 6, pages 60–73.

Flora, P., Kraus, F. and Pfenning, W. (1987) *State, Economy and Society in Western Europe, 1815–1975*, two volumes, London.

Forder, J. (1998a) 'The case for an independent European Central Bank: A reassessment of evidence and sources', *European Journal of Political Economy*, Vol. 14, pages 53–72.

Forder, J. (1998b) 'Central Bank Independence – Conceptual Clarifications and Interim Assessment', *Oxford Economic Papers*, Vol. 50, pages 307–334.

Forder, J. (1998c) 'Is the European Union really a Friend of Free Trade?', Politeia Lecture, December 15th 1998.

Friedman, M. (1968) 'The role of monetary policy', *American Economic Review*, pages 1–17.

Giavazzi, F. and Giovannini, A. (1989) *Limiting exchange rate flexibility: the European Monetary System*, MIT press, Cambridge, MA.

Gros, D. and Thygesen, N. (1991) *European Monetary Integration*, Longman, London.

Gros, D. and Thygesen, N. (1998) *European Monetary Integration: From the EMS to EMU*, London and New York.

Hummels, D., Rapoport, D. and Yi, Kei-Mu (1998, June) 'Vertical specialisation and the changing nature of world trade', *Economic Policy Review*, Vol. 4, No. 2, Federal Reserve Bank of New York.

IMF (1997, October) *World Economic Outlook*.

Johnson, C. (1996) *In with the Euro, out with the pound: the single currency for Britain*, London.

KPMG Management Consulting (1997) 'Europe's preparedness for EMU', Research Report.

Layard, R., Nickell, S. and Jackman, R. (1991) *Unemployment: macroeconomic performance and the labour market*, Oxford.

MacDougall, Sir D. (1992, May) 'Economic and Monetary Union and the European Community budget', *National Institute Economic Review*, National Institute of Economic and Social Research.

Mazower, M. (1998) *Dark Continent: Europe's twentieth century*, London.

Milesi, G. (1998) *Le Roman de l'Euro*, Paris.

Mundell, R. (1998, March 24th) 'Great Expectations for the Euro', *Wall Street Journal Europe*.

Nickell, S. (1997) 'Unemployment and Labour Market Rigidities: Europe versus North America', *Journal of Economic Perspectives*, Vol. 11, No. 3.

OECD (1994) *Country report on France*, Paris.

OECD (1995) *Country report on France*, Paris.

OECD (1997) *Country report on France*, Paris.

OECD (1998) *OECD Economic Outlook*.

Oppenheimer, P. and Forder J. (1996) 'The Changing Rationale of Monetary Union' in Hayward, J. (ed) *Elitism, Populism and European Politics*, OUP, Oxford.

Pennant-Rea, R. *et al.* (1997) *The Ostrich and the EMU: policy choices facing the United Kingdom*, Centre for Economic Policy Research, London.

Porter, R.D. and Judson, R.A. (1996, October) 'The location of US currency: how much of it is abroad?', *Federal Reserve Bulletin*, Vol. 82.

Ramaswamy, R. and Sloek, T. (1997, December) 'The real effects of monetary policy in the European Union: what are the differences?', International Monetary Fund Working Paper WP/97/160.

Redwood, J. (1997) *Our currency, our country: the dangers of European Monetary Union*, London.

Sachs, J. and Sala-I-Martin, X. (1992) 'Fiscal Federalism and Optimum currency areas: evidence from Europe and the United States', in Canzoneri, M., Grilli, V. and Masson, P. (eds) *Establishing a Central Bank: issues in Europe and lessons from the US*.

Samuelson, P. (1964, May) 'Theoretical notes on trade problems', *Review of Economics and Statistics*.

Szymanski, S. (1994, September) 'The City Labour market', in *The City Research Project*, Corporation of London.

Thygesen, N. (1998, May) 'EMU, Britain and other outsiders', Special Paper No. 102, Financial Markets Group, London School of Economics.

Vinals, J. and Jimeno, J.F. 'Monetary Union and European Unemployment', Documento de Trabajo No. 9624, Servicio de Estudios, Banco de Espana.

Von Hagen, J. (1992) 'Fiscal Arrangements in a monetary union: evidence from the US', in Fair, S. and de Boissieu, C. (eds) *Fiscal Policy, Taxes and the Financial System in an Increasingly Integrated Europe*, Kluwer, Dordrecht.

Index

BOTH SIDES OF THE COIN
THE ARGUMENTS FOR THE EURO

Is European monetary union going to usher in a new era of prosperity for Europe or will it precipitate financial meltdown? What will be the effect of euro on jobs? And on interest rates and mortgages?

The single currency fills the pages of the newspapers every day, but the arguments in favour of the euro are never set out clearly and concisely. Here, in an elegant essay by one of Britain's leading City economists, are the powerful arguments for joining the single currency as soon as possible. Christopher Huhne lucidly explains the arguments for the euro – cheaper capital, more transparency, lower transactions costs, greater economic mobility – and he shows why the disadvantages have been overstated.

Christopher Huhne makes the case for joining the euro persuasively and convincingly.

For the arguments against, turn this book over.

BOTH SIDES OF THE COIN

THE ARGUMENTS FOR THE EURO

by

Christopher Huhne

P

PROFILE BOOKS

First published in Great Britain in 1999 by
Profile Books Ltd
58A Hatton Garden
London EC1N 9LX

Typeset in Galliard by MacGuru
macguru@pavilion.co.uk
Printed in Great Britain by Biddles Ltd

A CIP catalogue record for this book is available from the British Library.

ISBN 1 86197 107 9

Contents

The author

Christopher Huhne, a long-standing economics commentator for press and television, is the founder and head of one of the largest teams of economists in the City of London. As group managing director of Fitch IBCA, an international debt-rating agency, he and his team research and rate around 60 countries that borrow on the international capital markets, including all the EU member states. A former council member of the Royal Economic Society, Christopher Huhne is a well-known speaker and writer on the implications of the euro, contributing articles to *Central Banking*, *International Economy* and *The Banker*. He is also an economic adviser to the Liberal Democrats, and was a member of the recent policy commission that suggested ways of preparing Britain for membership of EMU.

Until 1994 Christopher Huhne was business and city editor of the *Independent* and the *Independent on Sunday*, as well as writing a weekly economics column in the *Independent on Sunday*. He worked for the *Guardian* for ten years as both leader-writer and economics editor, and was previously Brussels correspondent of *The Economist*. In 1990 he won the financial journalist of the year award. His previous books include *Debt and Danger: the world financial crisis* with Lord Lever of Manchester, and *Real World Economics* and *The Ecu report* with Michael Emerson.

Preface and acknowledgements

This book is an argument about the most important political decision facing Britain today. With 11 countries adopting the euro on January 1st 1999 the debate will not go away. It has already split the Conservative Party, and it is a defining issue which has the ability to reshape old loyalties. In this context there has been a lot of low political debate, which has largely used whatever projectiles happen to be at hand. But there has been too little elucidation of the economic issues, although there could hardly be anything more economic than the decision on whether to adopt a new currency. We aim to fill the gap.

We have embarked upon the book in this form – in two halves, with a case for and a case against – to highlight the issues behind the decision. Although this is a polemic, it is also designed to ensure that any intelligent reader of a British newspaper is able to cut through the chaff in the debate and focus on the important points. We have, however, imposed certain rules on ourselves. The facts cited on each side in this book are not in dispute between us. What clearly differentiates us are matters of judgment; how much weight should be given to one factor or another.

Books of this kind owe a great debt to others which have gone before. Thanks are also due to colleagues who directly and indirectly helped to shape some of these arguments. Chris Huhne thanks Michael Emerson, with whom he wrote a previous book on the single currency dealing with the general arguments applicable to Europe as a whole. He would also like thank specifically John Arrowsmith, Andrew Duff, Will Hutton, Richard Portes, Lionel Price, Vicky Pryce and William Wallace for reading part or all of the manuscript and for providing many helpful comments and insights. James Forder would like to thank John Arrowsmith, Donna Bellingham, Ann Branch, Anand Menon, Malcolm Walter and, in particular, Peter Oppenheimer for reading the manuscript. They have helped both to excise many errors of fact and interpretation and to substitute clarity for muddle. Any problems that remain are, of course, ours.

Christopher Huhne and James Forder
December 1998

1 **Introduction and summary**

Whether you are for the single currency or against it, you cannot doubt the importance of the issue. The single currency that 11 member countries adopted on January 1st 1999 is the most important development in Europe's economic history since the foundation of the common market in 1958. If it works the euro will usher in a golden age of European prosperity. It will create a single economic space stretching from Helsinki in the north-east to Cadiz in the south-west, and from Sligo in the north-west to Brindisi in the south-east. Before long this area will encompass not only the 11 founding members – Belgium, France, Finland, Germany, Ireland, Italy, Luxembourg, the Netherlands, Spain and Portugal – but also Greece and the candidate democracies of renascent central and eastern Europe which will join early in the new century: the Czech Republic, Estonia, Hungary, Poland and Slovenia. Can Britain really stand aside?

Precisely because the euro represents such a significant change, it has driven a meat cleaver through the Conservative Party and created doubters in the Labour Party too. It is one of those political issues which arrive once every two or three generations with the capacity to divide former friends and remake tribal loyalties. The nearest parallels are Home Rule for the Liberal Party in the late 19th century and the repeal of the Corn Laws for the Tories in the mid-19th century. It has been a long time since such an important issue has forced British politicians to put their judgment of the national interest ahead of their commitment to their party, right or wrong. As a result, this debate stirs passions like few others. Equally, it obscures the real economic arguments. Money, after all, is ultimately a convenience: a means of exchange, a store of value and a unit of account. It is not a piece of national bunting to be waved like a flag. The idea that it should be a symbol is particularly bizarre, since the head of the British monarch did not appear on banknotes until after the Bank of England was nationalised in 1946.

Within the enormous euro area people will be able to do business with as few unnatural obstacles as exist within, say, the United States. They already have freedom of movement within the founding-member states and freedom to work in each others' countries. They also have freedom to buy and sell goods, services and investments in other member states. But at present those freedoms are inhibited because of the existence of different currencies. A sudden lurch in an exchange rate, such as the 15% jump in the value of the Japanese yen against the US dollar in a just a few days in early October 1998, can wipe out planned profits on an export sale or an overseas investment. In a stable environment European businesses will be able to deal with each other without worrying about a different currency. They will be able to focus on what matters in their business relationships: is this purchase good value, and can we make a profit on this sale? All the difficulties and risks of transactions which involve more than one currency will be removed. Thus far more business will be done, and more business means more prosperity and more jobs.

There is another effect: lower interest rates. The financial markets trust Europe's new central bank more than the Bank of England. As a result they believe that inflation will stay low. This means that savers are prepared to lend money at lower interest rates, and lower interest rates mean lower costs of debt service for borrowers, whether they be mortgage holders, businesses or the government. The French and German governments, for example, can borrow money at 1% a year less (over ten years) than the British government. If the British government could reduce its borrowing costs to their levels, as it would if it adopted the euro, it could save £4 billion a year. It could cut income tax by 2 pence in the pound, or raise public spending on health and education. A percentage point cut in mortgage rates would reduce the interest paid by the average mortgage borrower by £400 a year.

The global financial crisis which began in the summer of 1997 underlines the value of the euro. The 11 countries which are adopting the euro will, of course, be affected by the crisis. Their exports will suffer too. But they are quite well insulated against it. Speculators have not attacked their currencies in the way they certainly would have before the euro. Even the perennially weak Italian lira has glided smoothly into the euro as if protected by a giant helping hand, and the Finnish markka has been happily stable despite falling commodities prices hitting exports. Outside the euro zone the effects of turbulence can be clearly seen. For example, Norway, another commodities exporter, has had a much worse experience. It has had to raise interest rates seven times by a total of 4.5 percentage points to protect the krone, but even this served only to limit the fall in the currency to 7% between the beginning of 1998 and October 1998. This defence of the Norwegian krone, crucial to stop the explosion of import prices and inflation, weighs heavily on businesses and jobs – a familiar story to people in Britain who remember the sterling crises of old.

Britain, too, has suffered from instability but in a different way. Sterling was bid up and up by the financial markets as interest rates were raised. This rise in sterling has damaged Britain's exporters, particularly in manufacturing. Jobs are being cut. Industrial confidence has plunged and industrial business is heading for recession. But now sterling has started to come down almost as fast as it went up. In March and April 1998 the pound was worth DM3.03, an astonishing 34% more than its average level in 1995. At the time of writing this book in October 1998 the pound had fallen by more than 9% to DM2.75. Remember that a typical profit margin on a business sale is somewhere between 10% and 20%. This margin could be wiped out by such a scale of currency change. How can British businesses plan their exports or their overseas investments with this sort of volatility? It is by no means impossible for the decline in the pound to gather pace and turn into a rout; it has happened before. Then the Bank of

England would have to raise interest rates to stop the pound collapsing. All of this would be avoided if Britain adopted the euro.

Before considering the detailed benefits of the euro, it is necessary to take account of Britain's unique characteristics and, indeed, the unique characteristics of the British. Know your prejudices and allow for them. British people come to Europe with a lot of intellectual and cultural baggage, much of which is not at all obvious but is built into our linguistic infrastructure. There are, for example, only three European languages in which people talk about 'going to Europe' as if it were a different continent in the way the British do: English, Russian and Greek. This linguistic trait, a feature of countries and cultures that have often felt themselves on the edge of European development, puts a certain distance between us and our continental partners. We wish them well. But psychologically we preserve an element of reserve which says that we are not entirely of them. We may have been given our painting by Holbein and Van Dyck, our music by Handel and our great country houses by Palladio, but, despite the Channel Tunnel and modern aircraft, mentally we are still a storm-tossed sea journey away from our continent.

This is an understandable detachment given our island status. No other people in Europe have enjoyed such a long uninterrupted period without an invasion by a neighbour as the English have since 1066. (The Welsh, Scots and Irish have different experiences.) This may have bred a certain complacency, if not arrogance, among those who mistake geographical advantages for human superiority. It may also have meant that we have been able to enjoy certain luxuries denied to others, including a distrust of the state and a healthy and sometimes curmudgeonly belief in liberty. French Colbertism, the origin of the interventionism which remains more prevalent in France than in Britain today, was the natural consequence of a people without settled land frontiers, who needed an organised state with all its coercive powers to defend it. (And once those powers had been taken, they could of course be used not just in defence.)

Despite these geographical and cultural differences, English and then British history has always been involved with the European continent. As traders, the British bought cheaply in one place and sold expensively in another. London was the largest port of Europe's western seaboard. British merchants traded to the northernmost ports of the Baltic and far into the Mediterranean. British economists, Adam Smith and David Ricardo, were the first to explain the virtues of free exchange and free trade. London became one of the largest markets in Europe without artificial tariff barriers, which was a spur to the development of early manufactures. English, and British, interests were always defined by the desire to maintain the most open trading arrangements that we could persuade our continental trading partners to accept.

If these arrangements were threatened by a dominant continental power (whether Spain in the 16th century, France in the long 18th century or Germany in the 20th century), we were generally to be found, along with our gold, in the coalition of powers ranged against it. This was a decision based both on our trading interest and on the reality that we needed allies. Although today we have a similar population to that of France or Italy, we used to be much smaller than they were. At the time of the Congress of Vienna in 1815 England, Wales and Scotland had a population of just 12.9 million compared with 29.4 million in France. (By 1841 Germany's population was 33 million and France's was 34.2 million but that of England, Wales and Scotland was 18.6 million.)[1] These entanglements were deemed vital to our national interests, but they cost us dear. Few British families emerged from the world wars without personal loss. Nearly a million British people died in the first world war alone.

The irony of the history of British involvement with continental Europe is that now we have a set of institutions which accomplishes every objective we have always sought, and yet we approach these institutions with a suspicion bordering on paranoia. The European Union assures free trade. It ensures that the disputes arising between trading partners – about covert protectionism through the operation of national standards, about subsidies to businesses which make other businesses unprofitable – are subject to the rule of law, by means of treaties, council regulations and adjudication by the European Court, rather than to settlement by invasion and war. The single currency ensures that these arrangements will be so advantageous to the economic life of every participant as to be impossible to unravel.

Of course, some people argue that nationalist conflicts in western Europe since 1945 have been prevented not by the European institutions but by the fear of communism. This may well be true. Certainly, the fear of communism was a powerful stimulus in Europe's market-oriented democracies, making them take what were often tough decisions on defence and foreign policy. But the communist threat has now vanished. With the fall of the Berlin wall in 1989 Europe's rival nationalisms are on their own again, uninhibited by an external bogeyman. The conflicts in Bosnia and in Kosovo could be merely a foretaste for other inter-ethnic conflicts in central Europe and beyond.

Another feature of Britain's island status is its clean-cut linguistic and cultural borders (with the exception of Welsh-speaking areas of Wales and of Northern Ireland). We forget that there is virtually no such thing as a clear linguistic or ethnic border in Europe. A patchwork quilt of linguistic and ethnic minorities spreads untidily across almost every frontier. There are German-speakers in Belgium, the Czech Republic, Denmark and Poland; French-speakers in the Brussels enclave of Flemish-speaking Flanders and in Switzerland; Basques, Bretons and Italians in France; Basques and Catalans in Spain; and Austrians in Italy's Sud Tirol. Among future EU members there are substantial Hungarian minorities in Slovakia and Romania, Croats in Hungary, Hungarians in Croatia, and Italians and Croats in Slovenia. In the old days feudal monarchies, such as the Austro-Hungarian empire or the Ottoman empire, could impose a settlement of sorts on this diversity by means of coercion. But there is only one set of institutions that can make sense of this diversity today: European institutions which ensure the essential liberal freedoms and guarantee the essential minority rights. With communism gone the real test of the European Union's institutions may only now be beginning.

Yet British attitudes towards the European Community have, from the start, been marked by nothing but suspicion. The Messina talks of 1955 were to result in the Treaty of Rome of 1957 and the Common Market of the six original member states (Belgium, France, Germany, Italy, Luxembourg and the Netherlands). At those talks Whitehall took the view that the treaty would have no chance of being agreed, ratified or applied, and if it were it would be unacceptable to Britain. As we know the outcome was different, and the treaty proved to be acceptable to Britain shortly afterwards.

There were direct costs of that early episode of Euroscepticism which are relevant today, because we may be repeating the mistake. British companies did not participate in the first great wave of economic integration. Our trade was not redirected to our partners because we had to pay the common external tariff. Our businesses did not have to face the intensified competition of the new marketplace and therefore became less competitive in other markets. The average annual growth rate of GDP (gross domestic product) per head in the United Kingdom from 1960 to 1973 was 2.5% compared with 3.7% in Germany, 4.3% in Italy and 4.5% in France. Today we may miss the wave of opportunity and restructuring that is about to take place on the continent because of the single currency.

The second cost was just as severe. When a country joins the European Union it has to accept the laws that have been agreed by the existing member states. The negotiation is really about timing: how long will each side have to phase in these laws? In this context the failure to participate at the beginning meant that many important policies were put in place without any consideration of British interests, as Britain was not a member. These proved subsequently to be a substantial burden when we had to accept them. The most onerous was the adoption by the original six members of the high support prices of the

Common Agricultural Policy (CAP), which were subsequently to involve a particular penalty for the United Kingdom as a large net food importer having to pay higher prices for food imports.

The third cost of being late was the Common Fisheries Policy (CFP), agreed in 1970 on the eve of the potential membership of four important fishing countries (Denmark, Ireland, Norway and the United Kingdom). Based on the principle that all EU fishermen should have equal and free access to EU waters, the decision swung the Norwegian referendum against membership. British fishermen's interests were too small to influence the matter, and they were sacrificed to the greater national good. In the case of the CAP and the CFP these are costs which we still pay today as penance for our Eurosceptic short-sightedness about our national interests. Neither the CAP nor the CFP would have been there if we had joined at the beginning. As we shall see, there is a risk that the same thing will happen again with the single currency. Once again, we have no influence over the early institutional arrangements for a system that, almost certainly, we will eventually join.

British Euroscepticism landed us in trouble again at the time of our involvement with the European Monetary System (EMS), or exchange rate mechanism (ERM), which we eventually joined in 1990, 11 years after its launch. Throughout European economic history countries have preferred to have some fixed relationship between their currencies, for the simple reason that European states were comparatively small and therefore conducted comparatively large amounts of trade with each other. Even the biggest and most self-sufficient European countries trade twice as much with the rest of the world as the United States or Japan, relative to their national output, and the smaller European countries can have trade shares in GDP which are six times higher. The countries participating in economic and monetary union (EMU) export some 23% of their national output, whereas the United States exports just 9.5% and Japan exports 8.3%. So Europe does more than twice as much trade as the United States or Japan. This interdependence means that a particular fall in the exchange rate in Europe, resulting in a rise in import prices, has more than twice the effect on inflation in Europe as in the United States or Japan. Similarly, a rise in the exchange rate can affect twice as many businesses. However, half of this trade dependency is with other European countries. So European policymakers have traditionally, and rightly, put a premium on exchange-rate stability either on a worldwide basis or, if that cannot be arranged, within Europe.

Until the first world war this stability was provided by the gold and silver standards, under which currencies were convertible into gold or silver (or sometimes, confusingly, both). The 1920s were marked by a series of attempts to reinstitute the gold standard, followed by a period of free-floating exchange rates during the depression in the 1930s. This experience persuaded the market economies after the second world war to adopt a de-facto dollar standard through the Bretton Woods system, which lasted until the dollar devaluation of December 1971 and the collapse into free floating in March 1973. Bretton Woods, while it lasted, was highly successful, ushering in a period of unprecedented growth, investment, high employment and rising standards of living. Its breakdown came about largely because of excessive enthusiasm in the United States for financing its budget deficits and foreign asset purchases through printing money, which it assumed grateful foreigners would hold.

The collapse of Bretton Woods did not dull European appetites for stability. In March 1971 the European summit of heads of government approved the Werner Report advocating monetary union and a federated system of European central banks. Within a year of the dollar devaluation the Community had launched the snake, an attempt to link the European currencies in a stable relationship once again. But within four years the general turbulence in the exchange markets of the time, increased by the impact of capital flows from the first oil-price shock, shook the franc out of the system. It was reduced to the Deutschemark and the Benelux and Danish currencies.

The period of European free floating was short. By 1978

Germany's Chancellor Helmut Schmidt and France's President Valéry Giscard d'Estaing had begun to take up the suggestions of Roy Jenkins, then Commission president, for a new initiative to create a 'zone of monetary stability'. The EMS was launched in 1979, but again without Britain. At the time the fear among British policymakers was that sterling would become overvalued if we joined. Instead, we suffered another example of the law of unintended consequences. We stayed out and endured the largest overvaluation in post-war British economic history as high interest rates, strong oil prices and Margaret Thatcher's rhetoric buoyed sterling. The result was a worse recession in manufacturing industry, which is particularly affected by sterling because it trades so much, than in 1929–31. Manufacturing output fell by a fifth from its peak to its trough.

Britain's late membership of the EMS was a disaster both politically and economically. We missed the period from 1979 to 1983 when the exchange rates of the participants were realigned to make up for the differences in their inflation rates. If a country had an inflation rate 2% higher than others it would devalue its central exchange rate target (or parity) by 2% to compensate.[2] In this period the EMS was essentially designed to stop the financial markets' 'irrational exuberance'. We also missed the period from 1983 to 1987 when the fixed parities were moved to compensate for about half the difference in inflation, and the participants gradually squeezed inflation out of the system. We eventually joined, with a volatile exchange rate at a time of comparatively high British inflation, when other countries were trying not to move their exchange rates at all.

We also joined at a time when the EMS itself was coming under maximum strain. In a fixed exchange-rate system each participant has to have a higher interest rate than that of the country with the most credible track record of having a stable value, as investors naturally prefer to shift to the most solid currency. For a long time the most credible currency has been the Deutschemark. German unification imposed large costs on the German taxpayer, which the government quite rationally met through extra borrowing to spread the burden over future generations. This stoked up spending in the German economy, which in turn meant that the independent Bundesbank pushed up interest rates to stop demand running ahead of the economy's capacity to supply. Because German interest rates rose other countries had to pay a higher interest rate, even though they were not suffering from the problems caused by unification.

German unification was a shock to the central currency in the EMS, and it should have been the trigger for a move in European exchange rates, with the Deutschemark allowed to rise. But France would not allow the franc to devalue against the mark. The result was that the system was fragile when Britain decided to join. Then Britain joined without consulting its partners about the appropriate exchange rate, even though it expected their support. Britain joined in the wrong way, at the wrong rate and at the wrong time. In 1992 the pound was ejected by the markets following substantial losses of official foreign-exchange reserves in a botched attempt at intervention. Neither the then chancellor, Norman Lamont, nor the Conservative Party have managed to recover their previous reputation for economic competence. The voters assumed that the subsequent recovery happened despite the Tories, not because of them.

It would, however, be misguided to conclude that joining a single currency would be equally embarrassing. Consider the attack on the ERM from a European perspective rather than an insular one. Certainly, the exit of sterling and the Italian lira and the widening of the bands for other currencies were a debacle. The strategy of gradually aligning exchange rates until they seamlessly converged on monetary union – the final fixing – was undermined. But the objective of currency stability remained exactly the same for the same old reasons: if you do as much trade with your neighbours as most European countries do, you cannot afford to ignore your exchange rate in the way that the Japanese or the Americans do. So you do not go back to floating exchange rates. You look at other options.

Economic theory also told us that the ERM was likely to come under severe strain, and this was predictable and predicted.[3] It suggested that you could have two out of three of the following objectives: fixed exchange rates, an independent interest rate policy and free capital flows. But having all three at the same time would be a felicitous accident. During most of the post-war period, for example, there were restrictions on free capital flows in Europe which meant that countries were able to maintain their exchange-rate pegs to the dollar while setting interest rates according to national conditions. Once capital flows were liberalised, as they were in Britain in 1979 and in other member states such as France as late as 1990, short-term money could flow to take advantage of higher interest rates. Either those interest rates would have to come down to a level consistent with the interest rates of the other pegged currencies, or other interest rates would have to go up. Alternatively, the exchange-rate link would have to be broken. Monetary union (a single currency) merely represents the decision to have free capital flows and a fixed exchange rate, with the sacrifice of an independent interest-rate policy for each country.

It is in this context that the frequent British jibe that 'they are only doing it for political reasons' should be seen. This is frankly absurd. Politics and economics are intimately entwined. Nothing of any consequence in economic policy is ever undertaken except for political reasons, and these political reasons may indeed be the promotion of prosperity for potential voters. The single currency swam back on to the agenda in Europe, partly because of the realisation that fixed exchange rates were unlikely to be sustainable and partly because the alternative of free floating has traditionally been so disruptive. If EMU leads to greater prosperity, which in turn further binds together the member states of the European Union, is this an economic fact or a political one? It is surely both, and both objectives are desirable.

People and politicians who are in favour of monetary union may also be in favour of greater political integration in Europe. It is undeniable that French enthusiasm for monetary union grew in response to German unification after 1989 owing to the sheer size of the new Germany, a country of 80 million people compared with France's 58 million. But Chapter 5 will argue that there is no necessary connection between the two. There is no hidden agenda, only the agenda that has always been in the preamble of the Treaty of Rome for anyone to read. Eurosceptics frequently argue that because some German leaders are in favour of monetary union as a means to greater political union, this is proof that it must be so. But people can be in favour of things for all sorts of reasons, and this does not make them right. Ideas and arguments should be assessed on their merits, not because you agree or disagree with the motivations of the people putting them forward. Attacking people's motivations, rather than their arguments, is a rather disreputable intellectual technique formerly favoured by Marxists.

There are several examples of monetary unions without political unions, such as Luxembourg and Belgium since 1921. From 1921 to 1979 Ireland was in a monetary union with the United Kingdom, although no one would argue that this either undermined the Irish national identity or led to political union. Indeed, President Eamon de Valera redrafted the Irish constitution to stress the differences with the United Kingdom, but the monetary link continued. The Maastricht framework for monetary union will not undermine national identity or cultural diversity, which is one reason it stands a good chance of working without substantial amendment. If it does need amendment there will be a choice between devolving more power and responsibility to the participating states or giving this to the common institutions in Brussels. It will not be a foregone conclusion, and it will not necessarily involve centralising more power at the centre of a superstate.

The important point is not whether we will lose sovereignty by giving up the pound but whether we will gain some control over our economic environment that we would not otherwise have. Sovereignty is to be used to secure our national interests; it is not some iconic figure to be placed in a glass case with a 'Do not touch' notice on it. We know this instinctively in the context of defence. We pool our sovereignty

2 The advantages of the euro

This chapter sets out the advantages of the euro for all the countries that participate before turning to some specific advantages for Britain.

The euro is an extremely simple change: one currency replaces 11 national ones. But this event in itself entails a series of economic consequences, the nature of which only becomes clear on careful analysis. Much of the attention given to EMU concerns how it would affect the big decisions in the economy, such as interest rates and exchange rates. These macroeconomic effects are, of course, important. But critics of EMU often forget that its really important effects are likely to be on the small decisions made by thousands of individual companies. The real significance of EMU is that it makes markets work better in two fundamental ways. First, there are potential efficiency gains, such as the savings on the costs of exchanging one currency for another and their likely effects on growth. Second, there are the gains that can be expected from reducing risks, such as the risk that your investment or export order will be made unprofitable by an exchange-rate change. These reductions in risk also encourage investment and boost growth.

Efficiency gains

Lower transactions costs

An important, but as we shall see fairly mundane, advantage of the euro is that it cuts the costs of transferring money from one country to another. These transactions costs have been highlighted in the example of a tourist who travels through each European country in turn exchanging his original £100 for each successive currency. By the time he returns to the United Kingdom, without spending anything except the commission on exchange transfers, he will have only £53 left.[4] The remainder will have gone on exchange commission.

Of course, no one in the real world would ever be put in such a position, but the example highlights the substantial costs of the process which afflict every tourist and every business involved in exports or imports. Transactions costs – the commission charges and artificially unfavourable exchange rates which banks use in buying or selling foreign currencies – are worth about 0.4% of GDP (national income) in the European Union according to surveys undertaken by the European Commission.[5] As this is an average the figure is likely to be lower for Britain, because bigger countries do less trade than smaller ones. It may be no more than 0.2% of GDP. Some have argued that this is insignificant, but every improvement counts. Moreover, it is by no means the most important gain.

Easier price comparisons

In terms of efficiency, the most important advantage of EMU is in making prices easy to compare. In the period from January 1st 1999 to the summer of 2002 national notes and coin will continue to exist, even though legally they will be only an expression of the underlying euro. Many businesses will use price tags showing both the national currency and euros. But once these national notes and coin are replaced by the physical notes and coin of the euro, a process which will take place in the first six months of 2002, another important economic effect will come fully into play: it will be easy for consumers to compare prices across national markets. New competitive forces will be unleashed bringing new efficiency gains.

For small items that do not cost much this new competition is unlikely to matter. But for big-ticket consumer durables, ranging from cars to washing machines and televisions, this new ease of price comparison (so-called price transparency) is likely to have dramatic effects. Consumers, wholesalers and traders will naturally buy from the cheapest source, and in so doing they will put enormous pressure on companies to reduce prices and increase their competitiveness. If a company tries to rig the market by charging higher prices in one part of Euroland traders will soon start buying their goods in the cheaper parts and selling them in the more expensive parts. Price differences will become steadily less sustainable. This undercutting will benefit efficient producers, who will be able to take greater advantage of economies of scale. This ease of comparison is already scaring big companies into producing new price lists, which, for the first time, are the same throughout Europe. Multinationals will no longer be able to hide behind the veil of national currencies.

An example of where this effect may be important is the car market, where for many years substantial national price differences have continued despite the best efforts of the Commission and national competition authorities to reduce them. This is almost certainly because of anti-competitive restraints on trade, but the manufacturers justify the differences by blaming exchange rates. This would no longer be possible in EMU.

Table 2.1 Price comparisons for popular cars in EU countries

Car	Cheapest country	Most expensive country	% of cheapest	UK (% of cheapest)
Ford Escort	Portugal	UK	133.0	133.0
Ford Mondeo	Spain	Italy	127.7	123.9
Opel/Vauxhall Vectra	Spain	Germany	119.5	114.1
Rover 414	Ireland	UK	124.9	124.9
VW Golf	Netherlands	UK	130.9	130.9

Source: European Commission, DG 4.

The full significance of these price differences was dramatically illustrated in a recent study of the United States and Canada. This looked at price differences for products on each side of the US–Canadian border (and therefore each side of the currency divide between the US and Canadian dollars). It discovered that the border allowed prices for the same products to differ by a large amount; indeed, the cross-border price differences were equivalent to the price differences created by vast distances within a single market, with all the transport costs involved. Similar price differences for the same products within the United States and Canada occurred only at a distance of 1,780 miles.[6] So borders introduced substantial hurdles to traders despite a lack of trade barriers and (mainly) a common language.

Given that there are far more borders in Europe, the conclusion has to be that EMU would benefit consumers even more. It could, indeed, have similar effects to some of the great technological advances which have dramatically reduced transport costs, increased consumer choice and raised living standards. An example would be the introduction of the steamship on the North Atlantic in the late 19th century, which slashed the cost of shipping grain from the Midwest of the United States to Europe, and threw up enormous new business opportunities in both continents. EMU is a way of shrinking Europe, and bringing competing businesses far closer together to the great benefit of their customers.

Cheaper finance for businesses
The persistence of substantial price differentials is not confined to manufactured items. It also applies to some crucial services which have an important knock-on effect on the efficiency of other businesses, particularly banking. Indeed, some of the most exciting effects of EMU will be in this sector, which moves people's savings into the most efficient investment uses. The euro is likely to create cheaper finance for many companies and to open up new sources of risk capital for businesses that until now have been unable to raise money. The effect will be to make the European economy much more dynamic.

Different currencies matter more in banking and finance than almost anywhere else, as we can see from the limited progress that has been made in creating a financial single market. Indeed, the Commission's study of the price divergences within member states for standard banking products shows that they have actually increased since the launch of the single market. It is clear that the existence of loyal customer bases locked in separate national currencies has allowed some banks to raise charges disproportionately. The single market on its own appears to have had minimal effects in this important industry; only a single currency can make the single market a reality.

After EMU there will no nowhere to hide. Banks will have to become more efficient, reducing costs to compete in passing on the benefits to their customers. The process of consolidation has already begun. A Dutch bank, ING, has recently bought Belgium's Banque Bruxelles Lambert; Nordbanken of Sweden has merged with Merita of Finland; and there are persistent rumours that Germany's Deutsche Bank is looking for a big French partner.

This process of increased competition and consolidation among banks will particularly benefit small and medium-sized businesses, which are the customers most likely to shop around. Moreover, these businesses will also begin to benefit from another source of finance: the markets for shares and bonds. EMU will integrate the Euroland stock exchanges. Investors will want to compare pharmaceuticals or engineering companies wherever they are based in the euro area rather than German and Italian market levels. The comparison will be sectoral rather than national. As the shareholder culture takes root it will be easier for companies focusing on delivering shareholder value (in terms of increased dividends and capital gains) to raise new equity capital when they need it. This new shareholder culture fomented by EMU will also be a source of pressure on companies to become more efficient and profitable.

The bond market – the market in securities which pay an interest rate as opposed to equity securities whose dividends vary with profits – will also be a potent source of new finance. At present, the buyers of most bonds are naturally conservative. They want an assured return, and they look overwhelmingly to bonds issued in their own currencies. Indeed, many of them, particularly insurance companies and pension funds, have explicit rules which ensure that their assets (shares, bonds and so forth) are mainly in the same currency as their liabilities (the future pay-outs of insurance claims or pensions). This has constrained them to invest in their own national markets. Since January 1st 1999 they have been able to buy any securities in the euro area and still preserve this conservative policy of matching the assets and liabilities in their home currency. The ability to put together larger portfolios of bonds means that they are able to reduce the risk of holding them. In other words, investors can spread their eggs over more than one basket, reducing the risk of a problem. This means that they can afford to buy bonds which are individually riskier, even though the portfolio as a whole may be less risky.

This change in investor appetite for risk will be aided by the fact that most institutions will no longer be able to make money by playing Europe's currencies. Instead, there will be a hunt for riskier companies, which should in time find it easier to raise money for projects that would have been turned down within their national, segmented market. By encouraging risk-taking and entrepreneurialism the euro will also encourage the growth potential of Euroland. There is an enormous contrast between the types of borrowers that are able to raise money in a big, integrated capital market like the United States and the types of borrowers that are now able to raise money in the European capital markets split by national currencies. American investors have a much larger appetite for riskier bonds than European investors, and this helps get new ideas off the ground. In the United States 55% of all bonds are rated BBB and below. (This is a comparatively risky rating which means that there is at least a one in 20 chance of a default within ten years.) In Europe only 11% of all bonds are rated BBB or below.

Some gains, some losses
These are some of the reasons the most crucial benefit arising from the

single currency will be the opening up of vast, new and efficient markets. EMU provides the final keystone to complete the single market, and the single market cannot be a reality without EMU. Many will gain extraordinary rewards by providing new goods and services on a greater scale at a far cheaper price. But some are right to fear the outcome. The environment is bound to become more competitive. Some will lose and go to the wall. There will be some job losses, even if overall there are gains. But such costs will not last long.

Indeed, the effort to create a real single market in the late 1980s was widely expected to lead to job losses before it brought benefits. The opposite happened. Businesses anticipated the effects by increasing their investments. The result was an investment boom and an overall fall in unemployment. Although some people lost their jobs more new jobs were created, so that there was a net rise overall. Most crucially, however, economists know of no other way in which long-run prosperity can be increased other than through productivity and efficiency improvements of the sort that EMU should encourage. The important concern is not to protect specific jobs, but to ensure that the economy is dynamic and can create new ones. If we did not encourage such changes, we would still be taking the stagecoach to Bath and asking an ostler to rub down the horses. Every month the economy loses hundreds of thousands of jobs; the important objective is to ensure that it creates just as many or more than it loses. The only constant in economic life is change.

How far-reaching will these changes be? In traditional economic theory these gains from greater competition and market efficiency ought to be a one-off improvement in the way of doing things, even if they are spread over a number of years. In reality, however, such a one-off improvement in efficiency may have more lasting effects. They may become, in the jargon, dynamic gains. The most important point is that more output can be produced with a given amount of capital investment. This means that capital investment becomes more attractive to businesses, because the returns on capital have increased.

Capital investment will therefore rise. In the context of the European Union's single market 1992 programme, Baldwin estimated that the 'medium run growth bonus' might be half as much as the initial efficiency gains for Britain. With initial efficiency gains worth a minimum of 0.2% of GDP through savings in transactions costs, this would imply a further 0.1% a year growth bonus.[7]

There is another reason to expect that the market-widening and market-deepening impact of monetary union might improve growth. Traditional economic theory about growth assumes that it comes about because of technological innovation and that there are diminishing returns to investment (that is, the more you do the less you get back for each extra amount of investment). But the new growth theories point out that there may be increasing returns to investment for many businesses at many times. In other words, the extra profit on extra investment actually goes up. This happens, for example, because of constant overhead costs (such as investment in computer programmes) which would be a diminishing part of any increased output and sales. If this is so the growth impact of the single market, completed by monetary union, could be more substantial. It will allow European producers to reap substantial extra returns by producing on an altogether larger scale than they have done in the past.

Reducing risks

Less exchange-rate uncertainty

The replacement of national currencies immediately reassures everyone involved in foreign trade or investment with our European partners that they will no longer suffer sudden losses because of exchange-rate shifts. This is surprisingly significant. Even for countries participating in the ERM the monthly variability of the exchange rate has been more than 0.5% up or down. For countries outside, such as Britain, the monthly variability has been nearly 2%.[8] In other words, the random workings of the foreign exchange market may deprive a trader or an investor of that sort of difference. Remember that this margin is large compared with typical profits of 10–20% of the invoice.

This variability may reduce trade by generating uncertainty about the long-run level of the exchange rate, and it is one reason so many European businesses continually stress the importance of the exchange rate's stability separately from its level.[9] There are financial consequences as well. As a result of this uncertainty investors have often required an extra interest rate, a risk premium, on the securities of countries that are perceived to be at risk of devaluation. This was the case even when long-standing membership of the ERM had reduced actual variability (as in France, Belgium and the Netherlands for many years). This raises the real interest rate for everyone who borrows in that country, cutting off potential investment, jobs and growth.

Monetary union makes these risks, and interest-rate costs, vanish. It will dramatically reduce the risk of investing in another country within the union. It should therefore reduce the 'hurdle rate' or target rate of return which a business may require on its investment, and thus investment projects which are marginal today become possible under EMU. As a result some investments will be undertaken which would not happen under present circumstances. Investment should rise, and the potential growth rate of the Euroland economy should increase. Most importantly, this growth and investment should also allow a sustainable fall in unemployment. EMU should mean more jobs overall, even if some individuals and companies will be adversely affected.

This point about increased investment sometimes surprises people, because in theory businesses can insure, or hedge, against exchange-rate risks. But the forward and futures markets in foreign exchange are usually available for only a year ahead. This is enough to protect a trader, but even so the protection is imperfect and it costs money. Indeed, such an insurance policy can be a substantial part of a multinational company's financial costs. Moreover, it does not stop the underlying problem from occurring: you get a pay-out, but the house has still burned down. If the company has become uncompetitive in producing particular goods it will still be rational for the management to cut costs or production. The profit on the insurance policy may cushion the blow, but it will not avert the outcome. You cannot hedge (or insure against) costs. There are many examples of companies which have faced serious difficulties because of moves in exchange rates, including most of the manufacturing sector in 1979–81 and again in 1997–99.

These hedging problems are compounded when we consider a business that is thinking of investing in another country, rather than just selling to that country's consumers. It is possible, of course, for a big business to borrow entirely to make the investment in the currency of the country in which it is investing. Then if the currency drops the earnings flow and the value of the investment drop in terms of the company's home currency, but so does the liability (the borrowing) by an equivalent amount. This is a good insurance against the uncertainty of the exchange rate. However, only the largest companies are credit-worthy enough to be able to borrow to fund overseas investment in this way (and they rarely do so). More typically, companies are required by banks or by other lenders to put a substantial slice of equity finance into a subsidiary, and they may also lend money to it from head office. In these circumstances the company is clearly taking an exchange-rate risk.

By eliminating this risk such a company should be more willing to invest in other member states of Euroland. Business concepts that are successful in one member country should have the potential to be rolled out more rapidly in others. These business concepts usually come from the small and medium-sized businesses which are most affected by exchange-rate uncertainty today, and which are the most dynamic part of every economy. This is not a zero-sum game where one person wins what another person loses. A reduction in uncertainty will help everyone by boosting investment which would not be under-taken today. Investment will criss-cross Euroland, helping to revive areas which have fallen on hard times and where people offer their services more cheaply. What sort of impact could this have? Baldwin argues that there could be a reduction in the amount that businesses expect to compensate for risk (the risk premium) of about 1 percentage point, but that a drop of half a percentage point is a reasonable central estimate. A reduction in the risk premium of just 0.5% could lead to long-run increases in productive capacity and eventually in output of 5–10%, which is a very significant figure.[10]

These risk-reducing effects are, it is true, conjectural. Economists generally have been unable to find a large impact of exchange-rate uncertainty on trade flows, and there is no way of assessing the practical impact of the reduction in uncertainty and increase in returns for investment. We do not have past examples on which to draw. There are also many complicating factors, such as other uncertainties of product demand and competitors' strategies. However, this lack of ability to assess the impact is more likely to be a problem of economics than a problem of the idea. Surveys repeatedly show that businesses themselves thoroughly dislike the uncertainties associated with exchange-rate movements. For example, a recent survey of European businesses employing more than 5,000 people found that 87% of respondents expected to benefit from EMU and 58% cited reduced exposure to currency fluctuations.[11] Why would they say such a thing if currency swings were not a source of concern?

History also backs the euro. In the last period in which the world economy enjoyed genuinely fixed exchange rates (under the gold standard which lasted from 1880 until the outbreak of the first world war) the level of international investment was much greater than it is today. At that time there was no exchange-rate risk in investing in another country since almost all countries were committed to exchanging their national currency for a fixed amount of gold (or a currency like sterling which was in turn linked to gold). This meant that they could concentrate on the underlying risk of the investment without the worry and the false signals introduced by exchange-rate movements.

Table 2.2 on the next page shows the results. Capital flows as a percentage of national output (GDP) in the period 1880–1913 were far higher than they are today. The average annual inflow into Australia over that period was nearly 4% of GDP, almost double the scale of flows in the period 1965–86 to the largest recipient in the comparison. Canada was even more spectacular, recording nearly 8% of GDP inflows in each year, which is more than the amount in a single year which catalysed the Mexican crisis in December 1994 or the Thai crisis in July 1997.

Table 2.2 Capital flows under the gold standard compared with recent years (current-account balance as a percentage of GDP)

Gold standard 1880–1913		*Post-war 1965–86*	
Country	*%*	*Country*	*%*
Canada[a]	-7.7	Norway	-2.1
Australia	-3.7	Canada	-1.5
Sweden	-2.7	Belgium	0.0
Denmark	-2.6	Britain	0.0
Norway	-2.5	United States	0.0
France	0.2	Japan	0.7
Italy	0.6	Germany	0.9
Finland	1.6		
Germany	1.8		
Greece	3.1		
Britain	4.5		

a Average of data for 1900 and 1910.

Source: Tamim Bayoumi, International Monetary Fund, 1989.

Lower interest rates

This risk-reducing boost to investment may be compounded by a reduction in interest rates. If Britain joined there would be an immediate reduction in interest rates on all types of borrowing, whether borrowing linked to short-term interest rates (such as most variable-rate mortgages) or borrowing at long maturities and fixed interest rates. At the time of writing British short-term interest rates were 7%, compared with 3.3% in Germany and France. British ten-year interest rates (on government bonds) were 5.05%, compared with 4.05% in Germany. The cash saving for a £40,000 mortgage-holder of a cut to German levels would be £1,700 a year (£142 a month).[12] The government too would benefit. A saving of 1 percentage point a year on the financing costs of government debt would eventually build up. Once all existing debt of some £414 billion was refinanced, the government would save more than £4 billion a year, or some 0.6% of GDP a year. This is enough to cut the basic rate of income tax by 2 pence in the pound, or to increase public spending on education and health by substantial amounts.

These would be savings that borrowers make in cashflow terms, but of course these higher interest rates in part reflect the likelihood that Britain will have more inflation than the Euroland countries. (Indeed, the official target is 2.5% a year for price rises, compared with an indication of 0–2% in Euroland). Inflation erodes the value of debt over time, so part of the higher interest rates paid in Britain merely compensates lenders for the loss of their capital through inflation. Thus lower interest rates reduce borrowers' immediate costs, but they also mean that their debt erodes less quickly.

However, it is likely that, taking both effects together, borrowers will be a little better off because lenders at the moment extract a premium for uncertainty. Also British monetary institutions are less trusted than their European counterparts, despite the independence which has now been given to the Bank of England. This is not an opinion; it is a fact. You can see this by looking at the difference in the long-term interest rates in Britain and France or Germany. There is no difference in the creditworthiness of these countries. Their public finances are surprisingly similar (in terms of deficits and debt), and they are all rated AAA. But Britain pays an extra 1 percentage point a year to investors on ten-year bonds because they want a premium to compensate for the risks of inflation and devaluation. Investors do not trust Britain as much as France or Germany, and the difference is the commitment to keep inflation down. In economic jargon French and German institutions (the European Central Bank) are more credible.

If interest rates are lower should pensioners be worried about their income? Not at all. Their savings would not be eroded by inflation as they have been so often in Britain in the last 30 years. Moreover, pensioners with savings in bonds and shares should see further capital gains as lower interest rates make them look more attractive. Borrowers benefit from lower interest costs, but savers benefit from greater security and from capital gains on other investments. EMU benefits both savers and investors.

There should be another big benefit for both borrowers and lenders in the euro area: interest rates as a whole ought to be not only lower but also more stable. They will not be subject to the enormous swoops and surges that have bedevilled British interest rates over the last 30 years. This is partly because the framework for monetary policy in Euroland guarantees that political gerrymandering ahead of elections cannot happen. The people who decide interest rates are politically disinterested central bankers. (We will consider the political arguments on this issue in Chapter 5.) But it is also an effect of averaging. Euroland is a big area where some parts will be expanding rapidly while others are growing slowly. Because interest rates will reflect average monetary conditions throughout Euroland, they will be more stable than interest rates which reflected the ups and downs of the individual countries. Macroeconomic forecasters know this effect well from forecasting GDP (overall output) and its components (consumers' expenditure, investment and so on). GDP is much more stable than the components.

Fewer balance-of-payments constraints

There is one other growth effect which could be important. In the past there has been some evidence that governments become worried if a large difference develops between exports of goods and services and the corresponding amount of imports. Such a current-account deficit on the balance of payments has to be financed by capital inflows, and a rapid reversal or just a cessation of these flows can cause an unpleasant crunch. This, indeed, is what has happened in Asia over the last two years. The exchange rate weakens sharply or interest rates have to be raised sharply to hold the exchange rate. In this sense there may be a balance-of-payments constraint on growth because of the fear of the way in which the exchange market may react. By abolishing the internal exchange rate between EU member states this constraint on policymakers is lifted. Each member country has equal access to the foreign exchange generated by the collectivity. Growth can continue at its natural rate without interruption from a stop-go cycle. For Britain, which has long been bedevilled by perceived balance-of-payments weakness and by sterling crises, this could be a particular boon.

Putting numbers on these effects is extremely tentative, not least because the nitty-gritty of improving the efficiency of markets is less easy to quantify than grand claims about the effects of a cut in interest rates or a boost in public spending. But the microeconomic effects matter as the impact of trade liberalisation has shown. It is clear that the orders of magnitude are likely to be substantial. The European Commission has estimated a growth bonus of 0.7% a year[13] owing to efficiency gains alone, disregarding the reduction in risks. The range could be anything from 0.4% to 1% a year, a substantial amount given that the underlying trend growth rate of the European economy is a little more than 3% a year. However, it would be wrong to succumb to the numbers game. Many big changes in economics cannot be quantified but are crucial nonetheless. How, for example, can the impact of the creation of the Bretton Woods institutions in stabilising the world economy be quantified? Yet few doubt that they were essential contributors to the post-war boom in the 1950s and 1960s.

An idea of what even small gains from EMU might mean can be gauged from the following calculation. Assume that the benefits are just 0.25% extra growth a year, which has to be a conservative estimate. The wonders of compound interest mean that an extra 0.25%

growth a year, for someone on average earnings of £16,375[14] in Britain, soon cumulates to a substantial benefit. At a trend growth rate for the economy as a whole of 2.1% a year in real terms this should have gone up to £20,157 in ten years' time (at today's prices). Add an EMU bonus of 0.25% a year and the figure would be £20,656, a real rise of £499 or 2.5%. If it is double that the real rise would be nearly £1,000. EMU is not like winning the national lottery, but it is not negligible either. Even the slowest increase would be the equivalent to more than an extra year's pay increase every ten years. If the Commission is right it will be the equivalent of an extra year's pay increase every three years.

To summarise these arguments, first, EMU will increase efficiency. It will complete the single market. It will allow businesses to exploit opportunities on a wider scale and will lead to substantial efficiency gains not just through a reduction in transactions costs but also through increasing returns to large investments. The rate of return will therefore increase. Second, EMU will reduce risks. The monetary arrangements would reduce the risk of inflation in Britain (this, at any rate, is the markets' belief) and therefore there should be a reduction in the cost of capital. There will be a reduction in borrowing costs for people and for businesses. In addition, the abolition of exchange rate uncertainty will reduce the risks attaching to investment, and will therefore reduce the target rate of return that businesses seek. The reduction in the cost of capital, the cut in the target rate of return and the rise in the prospective rate of return will encourage investment. This will raise the trend growth rate of the EU economies. EMU will make us richer, quicker.

None of these arguments is controversial. All that a critic can say is that each point is doubtful and the effects may not be important. But this does not seem credible when there are so many arguments about microeconomic gains, all of which point in the same direction. It also belies what we know of economic history and success: that big, competitive markets breed more successful companies and higher living standards. The history of trade integration within the EU is testament to that. So is the success of the United States, which remains richer than any other comparable industrial country not because its monetary or fiscal policies have been pursued with greater dexterity (that is hardly the case) but because its continent-wide market has led to efficiency which no other country can emulate.

Other advantages

A new world currency

Apart from the growth and efficiency effects of the euro, there is also a more nebulous but potentially significant benefit in having a nascent world currency. First, the creation of Europe-wide deep and liquid capital markets, for both equities and debt securities, will make those securities more attractive to people outside the euro area. Many official foreign-exchange reserve managers, for example, hold a disproportionate amount of US government Treasury bills and bonds simply because of the attractive liquidity (the ease of buying and selling, even in bad times) of these New York markets. Asset managers have the assurance that they will always be able to get their money quickly if necessary. By contrast, European bond markets have been fragmented by national currencies and are less liquid and attractive. A portfolio shift towards euro markets might reduce the cost of funds for businesses still further.

A challenge to the dollar?

A second effect of the euro is likely to be that many people outside Europe will want to hold euro banknotes as a means of exchange and a store of value. The euro could well come to challenge the role of the US dollar in this area. The American government and the Federal Reserve (Fed) have done well over the years merely by selling dollar bills to foreigners, who have to tender real goods and services or other currencies in exchange. This seignorage (the revenue which arises from the right to print money) is fiercely protected by the Fed, which recently issued full-colour posters in Russian showing potential clients

Table 2.3 The United States, Japan and the EU: relative size and use of currencies[a] (%)

	United States	*Japan*	*EU*
Share of world GDP	20.7	8.0	20.4
Share of world exports (ex-EU)	15.2	6.1	14.7
Use of currencies in trade	48.0	5.0	31.0
Use of currencies in debt securities	37.2	17.0	34.5
Use of currencies in developing-country debt	50.2	18.1	15.8
Global foreign-exchange reserves	56.4	7.1	25.8
Foreign exchange transactions	41.5	12.0	35.0

a Latest available data for different dates.

Source: IMF, *World Economic Outlook*, October 1997.

how they could distinguish the new $100 bills from forgeries.

Foreign holdings of dollar bills accounted for more than half of all $375 billion in issue outside banks at the end of 1995 and provide annual savings of $10 billion–15 billion in interest on US Treasury securities. Without foreigners' willingness to hold stocks of greenbacks in their bedsocks the United States would have to pay interest on borrowing instead.[15] The European Central Bank is clearly interested in gaining market share in this area as it has decided to print an €500 banknote. (This is a regrettable decision since the note will be of limited use except to foreigners, Russian mafiosi among them, who like large-denomination folding stuff to facilitate cash trades.) It seems likely that the euro will gradually displace the dollar as a useful means of exchange, particularly in eastern Europe. European taxpayers will then begin to benefit from some of these gains.

The impact of more attractive securities markets and of a shift to holding the euro as cash should be that any putative deficit on Euroland's balance of payments will be even easier to finance. However, Euroland is currently running a surplus on the current account of the balance of payments and is a substantial net creditor (in that it owns more foreign assets than it has foreign liabilities), so this issue is academic at present. All participants will benefit from this strong balance-of-payments position even if they have traditionally been weak in this area.

Summary

The euro will make a reality of the single market and enable gains in efficiency, scale and specialisation. As a result it will increase prospective returns on investment. This is one of three mechanisms whereby investment, growth and jobs are likely to increase. The reduction of exchange-rate uncertainty is also likely to increase cross-border investment. More credible monetary institutions will reassure financial markets and reduce interest rates. This will reduce the cost of borrowing in Britain. The creation of Europe-wide capital markets is also likely to reduce the cost of funds for business expansion. This process may be boosted by both a shift of investors from dollar-based to euro-based assets and the advantages of issuing a currency internationally used as a means of exchange. For countries such as Britain, which have traditionally been bedevilled by balance-of-payments problems and sterling crises, the euro also offers the tantalising hope of unimpeded growth.

3 The disadvantages of the euro

Since this is the section of the book advocating the euro, you might expect to see a short chapter on its disadvantages. That it is comparatively long is a tribute to the ability of the British to look gift horses in the mouth and to be much better at pointing out small flaws than spotting big advantages. The critics are particularly blind to the real microeconomic benefits of EMU. It is noticeable that business people and business economists are much more aware of these advantages than the academic critics. Of course, there are disadvantages of the euro to place in the scales. But they are small and are likely to diminish over time. The balance of benefits and costs therefore weighs heavily in favour of our membership.

The critics argue that EMU either cannot work or will work badly because the European economies are too different to accept the same interest rate and the same exchange rate, which is an inevitable consequence of EMU. In their view, a one-size-fits-all monetary policy will lead to breakdown and disaster. In the jargon, they contend that Europe is not an 'optimum currency area'. However, this is largely based on a misunderstanding, because no existing country is an optimum currency area. Currencies have been adopted not because they suit particular regions that trade a lot with each other, but because of political boundaries that may originally have been drawn up on the whim of a medieval marriage settlement. Embarrassingly for the Eurosceptics, the father of this whole field of economics and of the idea of optimum currency areas, Professor Robert Mundell, recently backed Europe's adoption of the euro and accused his critics of misunderstanding him. He argued that the euro's benefits would clearly outweigh the costs.[16]

Loss of an independent monetary policy

This chapter will show that the differences between euro regions are within the bounds that exist in other monetary unions, such as the United States, Germany and Britain itself. If a monetary union for Europe is inappropriate, then a monetary union is also inappropriate for parts of Britain, notably Northern Ireland and East Anglia, and there should be separate currencies for different parts of Britain too. But this would be a nonsense. The benefits of a separate monetary policy – of a separate national interest rate and exchange rate – are more limited than often supposed, and they have on several occasions proved to be a disadvantage.

Imagine that some economic shock hits Britain, or any other country within the euro area, and not the other parts of Euroland (in other words, the shock is asymmetric). Let us assume that a health scare hits British food production at the same time as a terrorist outrage hits tourism. People are thrown out of work. We need to boost other parts of the economy to increase the jobs to replace those lost in food and tourism, and we need to increase our exports to pay for the same level of imports. Nowadays, the Bank of England might simply cut interest rates and allow the pound to fall. Both movements would help the economy to adjust to the change in circumstances.

In principle, the loss of an independent monetary policy is a disadvantage in these circumstances. But how likely are these different shocks? A substantial amount of work has been done on whether the European economies behave in a similar manner to each other. The pioneering research in this field compared changes in output (GDP) in each country with changes in output in Germany, which was taken as the core part of Euroland since it represents about one-third of total output. It then looked at the extent to which these GDP changes matched over a long period of years, the so-called coefficient of correlation. As a simple rule of thumb, a correlation coefficient of more than 0.5 suggests a reasonable fit. The results, recently recalculated for a bigger group of potential participants, suggested that Austria, Belgium, Denmark, France, Greece, the Netherlands and Spain were all closely aligned with Germany over the period 1964–90.[17] However, Finland, Ireland, Italy, Portugal, Sweden and the United Kingdom all had correlation coefficients below 0.5. In the United Kingdom's case it was just 0.19.

Superficially, this finding does not look good for Britain's membership. The correlation is clearly lower than for any other country over the period 1964–90. But this has to be put into context. The first important piece of evidence is from other monetary unions. In the United States the correlation coefficient between the Mideast and other regions was also below 0.5 in the case of the South-west and the Rocky Mountains. Indeed, the Rocky Mountains area had a correlation coefficient of just 0.18, a little lower than the similarity between Britain and Germany. Other monetary unions survive and prosper even when some parts of them are as different from the core area as Britain from Germany.

In one important respect this type of study does an injustice to both the European and the US monetary unions because it implicitly assumes that the monetary authorities set interest rates for a core area and ignore the rest. A crucial advantage of EMU over the traditional European fixed exchange-rate system revolving around the German Bundesbank's decisions is that the European Central Bank (ECB) will take account of developments throughout the region, not just in Germany. Therefore the real test of appropriateness should be whether GDP growth moves in line with the average, not with some other part. This has been calculated for three different periods by the Organisation for Economic Co-operation and Development (OECD) and is shown in Table 3.1 opposite.

These figures show that the European economies move closely in line with each other, apart from in the middle period (1987–92H1) when Germany was out of line with the average. (Denmark moved in the opposite direction to the average at that time.) The reason for the divergence was Germany's unification in 1989. At that time the

Table 3.1 GDP growth correlations with the prospective euro area

	1977–86	1987–92H1	1992H2–96
Germany	0.89	0.28	0.93
France	0.72	0.85	0.99
Italy	0.93	0.65	0.92
Austria	0.65	0.71	0.85
Belgium	0.51	0.92	0.97
Finland	0.17	0.68	0.88
Ireland	0.30	0.65	0.76
Netherlands	0.76	0.60	0.89
Portugal	0.48	0.43	0.41
Spain	0.21	0.62	0.94
United Kingdom	0.48	0.53	0.57
Denmark	0.33	-0.07	0.54
Greece	0.65	0.36	0.83
Sweden	0.27	0.61	0.90

Note. Correlations are based on semi-annual data and are with the EMU 11 area.

H stands for half.

Source: OECD secretariat.

German economy was being boosted by an expansionary fiscal policy as the government decided that some of the costs of unification should be met by borrowing and therefore shared with future generations. This put pressure on the Bundesbank to raise interest rates to offset the impact on demand, which caused other European countries to raise their interest rates to keep in line with the Deutschemark.

If the euro had been operating there would have been no such rise in interest rates (although Germany would have suffered overheating and extra inflation instead). The real point, though, is that German unification is the sort of economic shock which, by definition, will never happen again. It was a one-off, and it would be foolish to construct monetary arrangements on the assumption that such shocks will frequently occur given the other advantages of a single currency. If we look at the other periods the correlations look surprisingly high, although they do break the Euroland area into a group of countries that move together strongly (Austria, Belgium, France, Germany, the Netherlands and, surprisingly, Italy) and the others.

European economies are becoming more integrated

There is one other message from this research: it is clear that the European economies are moving together more often today than used to be the case. This is not surprising. As we shall see, the European economies are becoming steadily more integrated with each other. It is noticeable that Britain no longer looks as lonely as it does if compared merely with the German economy. Britain and Euroland as a whole move together quite happily, and the links are increasing. Thus a single interest rate and exchange rate are likely to become ever more comfortable for the United Kingdom. Moreover, this work underestimates the ease with which Britain would fit into the euro because the correlation is calculated with the average of the 11 rather than the 12, as it would be with Britain as a member. If Britain joined, European monetary policy would take account of monetary conditions in Britain as well as elsewhere.

There is another way of thinking about how appropriate the euro would be, which is to look at the diversity within the euro area compared with the diversity between regions within existing member states (or effective monetary unions). Here the surprising result of some interesting new research is that, for Germany and Britain, the correlation with Euroland as a whole is likely to be as appropriate as the monetary unions which exist now between national regions and their national economies.[18] For example, Britain's economy is more closely linked with Euroland than either East Anglia's or Northern Ireland's economies are with Britain. If Britain is thought to be too divergent to participate in the euro then the same logic would suggest that there should be separate currencies for East Anglia and Northern Ireland. The study shows that British regions are no more divergent from the Euroland average than German regions, with the sole exception of Northern Ireland.

My overall conclusion from these studies is that Britain may have to adjust more than the core countries, and may therefore lose more than some other potential participants from the loss of a separate interest rate and exchange rate. Britain is not part of the core group for which a common interest rate and exchange rate is likely to prove most comfortable, and there may be periods in which European monetary policy is inappropriate for British needs. But the loss is well within the bounds already shown to be practicable by the experience of both the United States and Britain's own regions. It would also be handsomely offset by the other benefits likely to arise as a result of our membership of the euro.

Different cultures are not a barrier to monetary union

James Forder airily dismisses all this research as irrelevant on the grounds that, however well integrated are Europe's economies, Europeans simply do not have the fellow feeling which will allow periods in which European interest rates or the euro exchange rate will be inappropriate. This vastly overestimates the extent to which interest rates are likely to become a political issue, a misjudgment which is understandable given Britain's sad inflationary and interest-rate history. When inflation is high and rising, interest rates have to be higher and to rise faster. But this view is far too pessimistic for countries with reasonably low inflation and stable interest rates. Euroland will be, in this respect, much more like Germany than Britain. Interest rates will not vary much, and they will therefore not become a political issue in the way they have in Britain.

We also have many examples throughout the world of countries composed of substantially different cultural and ethnic groups which are nevertheless in a monetary union. Within Europe, Switzerland is a stable monetary union despite its four language groups and independent cantons. Belgium has three languages and shares a currency with Luxembourg. Outside Europe there are more examples. China has many different languages, albeit sharing common written ideograms. India has more than ten major languages and two language groups as different as romance and teutonic languages in Europe. South Africa contains speakers of Xhosa, Zulu, Afrikaans and English. All of these multi-ethnic societies survive more or less happily with a single currency.

Trade patterns

Moreover, all the work on the linkages between the European economies, on which we can base a judgment about the applicability of a common monetary policy, is based on past history which underestimates the growing linkages between the European economies. In Britain's case, for example, the trade share of GDP with other EU members rose from 3.3% of GDP in 1960 to more than 12% in the mid-1990s. This increasing integration is being reinforced by a change in the nature of trade. Traditional trade has been in products where countries have particular advantages; for example, Scotland exports whisky and buys bananas from the Windward Islands. In both cases the production process is almost exclusively in those countries, which makes them independent of each other and liable to differing external shocks. A blight on the banana crop would not affect Scotland at all.

But modern trade is increasingly about trade among businesses in the same industry. German and Swedish car makers buy components from British-based Lucas and GKN, Sony buys components from Thomson of France to make televisions in Wales, and so on. These trends have made the structure of all developed economies, particularly the European economies because they are more integrated, more similar over the years. Developed economies are becoming less prone to shocks which will define the fortunes of one compared with another. A shock which affects the European car industry – say, a sudden shift in consumer tastes towards Detroit-produced gas guzzlers – is likely to affect Euroland fairly evenly. In these circumstances one monetary policy – one interest rate and exchange rate – can help make the adjust-ment that is necessary. A recent study shows that such intra-industry or vertical trade was slightly higher in Britain, at 19.1% of total trade, than in Germany (at 16.3%) or France (at 18.7%). All the European economies were much more vertically integrated than the United States (7.4%) or Japan (6.6%). In all cases vertical trade had been increasing sharply.[19] So there are sound reasons for believing that the extent to which the European economies will move together will grow, even without the additional incentives of the integration brought about by the euro itself.

Nor is the existing structure of external trade much different among the larger member states. The most common way of looking at the structure of trade is to examine the proportion of exports that go to particular destinations, and this shows that Britain's share of exports outside the euro area is some 52% compared with Germany's or Italy's 48%. However, the more significant measure of a country's exposure to developments in a particular region of the world is to look at its exports to that area as a proportion of total output. After all, it does not much matter if a country exports a high proportion of its exports to a particular country if its exports are actually an insignificant part of total output. Table 3.2 shows trade outside and inside the Euroland-12 (assuming Britain is included) compared with GDP is surprisingly sim-ilar for the big member states. Britain is less exposed to non-Euroland trade than Belgium, Finland, Ireland or the Netherlands, all of which are first-wave members.

Britain's exposure to exports outside the euro area – the supposed risk that Eurosceptics claim makes Britain uniquely unsuited to share a currency with the other participants – is in fact only a little higher than the average. The exposure of Britain is remarkable more because it is so similar to the average. Within the total of exports outside the Euroland

Table 3.2 Export exposure to euro area and outside[a] (% of GDP, 1996)

	Non-euro area exports	*Euro area exports*
Ireland	24.9	45.4
Finland	18.8	12.2
Belgium/Luxembourg	18.2	42.6
Sweden	17.4	16.4
Denmark	12.7	14.3
Netherlands	12.0	33.2
United Kingdom	11.6	10.9
Germany	10.6	11.3
Euro-12	**10.2**	**13.9**
Italy	10.0	10.7
Austria	9.7	15.6
France	7.5	11.2
Spain	5.5	12.0
Portugal	5.4	18.1
Greece	3.2	3.8

a Euro participating countries plus United Kingdom, as if it were a Euroland member.

Source: IMF, *Direction of Trade statistics*; *International Financial Statistics*.

area the only significant difference is that Britain exports more to the United States and less to other non-Euroland markets. Britain's exports to the United States account for 2.7% of GDP, whereas the Euroland-12 average is 1.7% of GDP. But this is hardly a significant difference within the overall picture of similarity. Of participants in EMU, Ireland has a higher proportion of GDP going to the United States in exports, and both Finland and Belgium have shares similar to that of the United Kingdom.

THE ARGUMENTS FOR THE EURO

The nature of debt

Another much-cited difficulty for the euro in general, and for Britain in particular, is the different nature of the debts which exist in different countries. Critics say that British households are more indebted than those on the continent, and that they generally borrow at short-term interest rates. Therefore they will bear the brunt of any adjustment in European monetary policy if Britain joins. If the ECB needs to tighten policy British households will feel the pinch soonest, because their mortgage rates are linked to short-term interest rates. The most recent comparison by the Bank for International Settlements, which is rather out of date, does indeed show that the interest rates on British debt are linked to short-term interest rates. About 90% of British borrowing in 1993 was at variable interest rates, compared with only 36% of German borrowing and 13% of French borrowing.[20]

However, this is not the end of the story. An interest-rate rise hits borrowers but benefits savers, and the impact on the economy as a whole depends on the balance of savers and borrowers. British households overall are net recipients of interest payments. In general, of course, younger people are borrowers and older people have financial assets. Since the spending of younger people with borrowings is more likely to have to fit their income, an interest-rate change is more likely to affect their spending than the spending of older people. So a rise cuts consumer spending and a fall boosts it. Interest rates also affect the corporate sector and its investment intentions. But the balance has to be carefully assessed to see whether an interest-rate change actually affects Britain more dramatically than other countries. You cannot merely assert that Britain would be worse affected by interest-rate changes because it has more variable-rate debt.

There have been several attempts to assess the true situation, and they do not support the simplistic view that variable interest-rate debt could be bad news for Britain in EMU. In a recent analysis the IMF suggested that a 1 percentage point interest-rate rise leads to a fall in output of 0.7–0.9% from the baseline projection of output in Austria,

Belgium, Finland, Germany, the Netherlands and the United Kingdom.[21] The low point is 11–12 quarters after the tightening. In the other group of countries (Denmark, France, Italy, Portugal, Spain and Sweden), a 1 percentage point tightening leads to a smaller but more rapid decline in output; the drop is 0.4–0.6% after 5–6 quarters. The most recent study at the time of writing, which encapsulates some important methodological advances, is by Professor Rudi Dornbusch and various colleagues. It suggests that there is actually rather less effect of changes in interest rates in Britain than in some other countries.[22] (Previous studies assumed that interest rate changes would affect the individual European economies as they have done in the past, including any effect on their exchange rates relative to other European countries. In EMU, of course, the interest rate will not affect the exchange rate with other EMU participants.) Indeed, their estimates suggest that the British economy will respond only two-thirds as much as France or Germany and only half as much as Italy. This is entirely contrary to the simplistic view that variable-rate mortgages will be a problem for the United Kingdom in EMU.

The evidence, therefore, is that the behaviour of the British economy when interest rates change is not much different from other member states. (As often happens in contentious areas of economics, the differences in the results of different models applied to the problem are more significant than the differences in the countries within each study.) Nor is EMU likely to prove problematic, even for British individuals with high variable interest-rate debt, because interest rates are likely to prove less volatile, as we saw in Chapter 2. It is also worth remembering that the particular dependence of Britain on short-term interest rates came about in response to high inflation. (This meant that lenders would not be prepared to lend unless there was some assurance that interest rates would move in line with inflation.) The move to EMU is likely to provide strong incentives for people to undertake borrowing at fixed interest rates for longer periods, because long-term interest rates will be lower than they are today and the ECB offers a credible commitment to low inflation in future.

Fiscal transfers

Critics of EMU also point out that there is no automatic mechanism to transfer money from parts of Euroland that have not been affected by a shock to the part that has. In their view this means that the social and political strains on EMU could become intense. In other monetary unions, notably the United States, the federal tax system has the effect of cushioning problems in part of the monetary union. When Texas suffered from the fall in the oil price in 1986 it paid less income tax to Washington and it also received transfers from Washington, which pays unemployment benefit. These offsetting fiscal transfers have been estimated, in the first instance, as worth about 30 cents in every dollar of income lost in the region.[23]

However, this point ignores the fact that someone has to pay for these transfers, and unless a region is particularly unlucky compared with other regions it will be paying higher taxes to provide such insurance for other regions. Moreover, it will pay higher taxes to pay its own transfers if they are funded through an increased budget deficit. Some two-thirds of the 30 cents in the dollar which are immediately handed back to the depressed region in lower income tax receipts and higher unemployment benefit are actually just a transfer to the region today, at the cost of higher taxes over time paid by the region itself. They are an inter-temporal transfer (a transfer from future generations to the present generation by means of borrowing) not an inter-regional transfer. Only 10 cents in the dollar is genuine insurance to more volatile regions.[24]

This is highly significant because countries are already in a position to borrow to cushion the impact of a short-term downturn. So two-thirds of the effects of the US federal system are already available through normal countercyclical borrowing. Moreover, part of the insurance function will continue to be performed within national member states by their own fiscal transfer systems. This now accounts for about half of the insurance potential of a Europe-wide system, further reducing the need for a fiscal federation.[25]

There could, of course, be a problem. What if the EU rules stop countries from borrowing? The ability of fiscal policy to offset shocks that hit only one country depends crucially on the room for manoeuvre participating member countries have within the constraints of the Maastricht Treaty and the Stability and Growth Pact.[26] This essentially commits participants to a 'medium-term objective of budgetary positions close to balance or in surplus', which will allow member states to deal with normal cyclical fluctuations 'while keeping the government deficit within the 3% of GDP reference value'. If countries exceed a deficit of 3% of GDP, save in exceptional circumstances such as a fall in GDP of more than 2%, the Council of Ministers can levy refundable deposits (transferable into fines after two years for persistent offenders). These are equivalent to 0.2% of GDP plus a variable component of one-tenth of the difference between the deficit and 3% of GDP up to 0.5% of GDP.

It is true that these penalties may not bite as hard as some people think. They are subject to a decision by the Council of Ministers, voting by a weighted two-thirds majority of participants except for the member state concerned. Ministers may prove more reluctant to discipline their peers than the rules allow if they think that they might be next in the dock. In the wake of the election of a centre-left government in Germany and centre-left governments in most other member states, there may even be a more explicit relaxation of the rules to allow governments to spend money on infrastructure investment. But there is clearly a danger, on present rules, that a member state whose budget position is not close to balance at the beginning of a recession may be forced to take fiscal measures which will actually aggravate the downturn rather than cushion it.

If Europe does not relapse into recession this danger looks containable, because of the starting position of participating countries' budgets. The strength of the underlying budget position of the participating members has been underestimated by many analysts, who have pointed to the various one-off measures, the so-called fiddles and fudges, used to flatter the figures in 1997 in order to meet the 3% criterion for membership. Everybody was at it: the French paid a special dividend from France Telecom; the Italians had a euro tax; and the Spanish even changed from cash to accruals accounting (enabling them to book tax revenue due rather than just tax revenue paid).

However, these one-offs were applied to budgets which were, for the most part, still depressed by recession-hit tax revenue and high welfare payments. In time the upturn in the European economies should boost tax revenue without any change in tax rates, and welfare spending should ease as unemployment falls. If adjustments are made for these cyclical factors the budget balances of the member states in 1998 were already near the level necessary to stay within the 3% limit, even in a normal recession. For example, Italy probably needed additional fiscal tightening of just 0.2% of GDP to move the underlying budget position to such strength that it would be able to withstand a normal recession and keep the total budget deficit within 3%. This was an insignificant amount given that taxes have risen and public spending has been cut by some 9.5% of GDP since the Amato administration began work.[27] Only Germany, Finland and Portugal have significant fiscal tightening of more than 0.5% of GDP still to come. In the case of Britain the budget position was already strong enough to withstand a normal recession and stay within the limits. So in principle we should have no difficulty in meeting the criteria. Nor should we have problems staying within these criteria in a normal recession.

Exchange-rate flexibility and devaluation

Although fiscal policy will continue to have a primary role in cushioning the impact of changes in the economic environment for regions (or for countries), it is not in itself a means of adjustment. It is a way of delaying and making more palatable the changes which may be necessary to adapt to changes in consumer demand or supply changes (such as competing goods which substitute for long-established ones). The adjustment ultimately has to be made by businesses and by their work-forces. If an economy as a whole suffers from an adverse shock, whereby its capital and labour are underemployed, it can at present use its exchange rate to help to price those unemployed resources back into work. A fall in the exchange rate makes exports cheaper when con-verted into foreign currency and imports more expensive in the home currency. The loss of the exchange rate is therefore a potentially impor-tant loss for countries which participate in EMU.

However, the usefulness of exchange-rate flexibility is heavily cir-cumscribed. Devaluations work only if they lead to a fall in the cost of production in the devaluing country even after allowing for subse-quent price rises. They can work when there is substantial unemploy-ment dampening down wage demands; this was the story of the sharp devaluation of the pound after its exit from the ERM in 1992. However, most devaluations in Britain have not worked except in the short run. The subsequent rise in import prices has pushed up domestic con-sumer prices, and the trade unions and powerful groups of employees with scarce skills have rapidly won wage increases to offset these price rises. Within a fairly short period domestic prices have risen by enough to compensate for the original fall in the exchange rate. What you gain on the devaluation roundabout you rapidly lose on the inflationary swings. Devaluation buys only a short-term gain.

This ratchet – devaluation, rising import prices, rising inflation, rising wage increases, more devaluation – is why the pound has fallen so far over such a long period of time since the 1960s, while having a negligible beneficial effect on the competitiveness of British goods in home or foreign markets. As Professor David Currie has pointed out:

> In 1966 sterling traded at about DM11. An independent mone-tary policy had allowed this to slip to around DM2.3 in 1996, an average depreciation of nearly 5% a year over 30 years. Monetary freedom has offered little real benefit to the United Kingdom; the

principal result has been that it has experienced on average nearly 5% more inflation than Germany. Moreover, the UK economy has exhibited greater instability over this period than any of its major competitors.[28]

This finding on instability is particularly interesting because it is quite likely that the operation of an independent monetary policy has actually aggravated Britain's problems. Certainly, the pursuit of strict monetary targets in the period 1979–81 helped to impart a serious economic shock to the economy. The Barber boom and then the reaction to the 1973–74 oil-price shock were also subject to widespread criticism, leaving Britain with a far higher inflation rate than its competitors. So it would be wrong to see monetary policy and devaluation solely as a way of helping to respond to adverse shocks. The operation of monetary policy in Britain has actually been a significant source of such shocks. The cure has sometimes proved worse than the disease. Combined with the increased incentive for governments elected under winner-takes-all election systems to use economic levers to secure their re-election, this is probably the main explanation of why Britain's economy has been the most volatile of all the leading seven industrial countries.

Over time the usefulness of the devaluation option, even if it is operated positively and helpfully, is also being eroded. As an economy becomes more open to trade the impact of a fall in the exchange rate on domestic inflation becomes more widespread. The pass through from import prices into inflation is more rapid, and the result is that devaluation becomes less effective. Monetary sovereignty is therefore a diminishing benefit in a world where economies are becoming steadily more integrated and dependent on each other. This is a lesson that the small economies learned many years ago. But it is increasingly true of the medium-sized European economies as well. To sum up, therefore, the devaluation option can be useful in extreme circumstances. But it can also prove to be a temptation which is overused, and which can lead to more problems than it solves.

It is easy to overstate the usefulness of devaluation even in extreme circumstances when there is substantial unemployment (as there was in Britain in 1992, for example). Professor Niels Thygesen has pointed out that the size of the real devaluation (after allowing for offsetting rises in domestic prices) needed to cut unemployment by 1 percentage point is surprisingly large. Typically, computer models of medium-sized European economies estimate that exports increase by about half as much as the fall in the real exchange rate over a two to three year period. With exports worth about one-third of GDP this implies that it would take a 20% real devaluation to produce an increase in output of about 3%. Yet this is the sort of increase needed to cut unemployment by 1 percentage point.[29] Thygesen concludes that his calculation suggests 'that giving up the use of exchange-rate changes makes only a modest difference to the macroeconomic performance of the EU economies'.

Labour markets and unemployment

Within monetary union the devaluation option is ruled out. So the only means of adjustment to changes in economic circumstances is through product, labour and capital markets. This essentially means labour markets, because businesses generally run down production or move elsewhere if their profitability is hit. So an adverse shock to the demand for products leads to the need for cost-cutting, which means cuts in the cost of labour (whether wages or jobs). Wages are businesses' biggest cost, and this effect is unavoidable. (Many business people question this, and say that wage costs are only a tiny part of their total costs. But they are not counting the wage element in the components and services that they purchase.)

The adjustment comes through labour markets. Either wage increases can respond quickly to unemployment, giving businesses an incentive to hire more labour, or the unemployed can move; in Norman Tebbit's phrase, the unemployed can 'get on their bikes'. In the United States labour mobility is much higher than in Europe. If a region becomes depressed or opportunities begin to wilt, people simply move to more prosperous and dynamic parts of the country. In Europe labour mobility is much lower than in the United States even within member countries, let alone between them with all the additional language problems that a cross-national move implies. A study which looked at net migration among the 50 states of the United States by comparison with the 64 regions of the European Union found that the average proportion of the population that moved each year in Europe was 0.2%, compared with 0.7% in the United States.[30] Americans are mainly, after all, Europeans with the travel gene. Europeans seem to like staying put, as was graphically illustrated recently by a genetic study which matched the DNA in a Cro-Magnon man's skeleton found in the Cheddar Gorge to a descendant teaching at the local primary school.

However, the Eurosceptics are wrong to argue that Americans' willingness to move region is a crucial way of making their monetary union work. Americans do not move around according to highs and lows in different regional economies, happily offsetting rises and falls in the unemployment rate. They move because many of them do not like the cold and the rain in the North-east and Midwest, preferring the sunshine of Florida, Texas and California. These movements of population are long-term shifts, and are not related to short-term movements in the business cycle.

So the only effective means of adjustment in monetary unions (including the United States) is real wage flexibility. Do real wages (that is, wages after allowing for the price level) adjust? The rough answer in Europe, including Britain, is that the labour market does not adjust rapidly to changes. Because employees may resist accepting a cut in the real value of their wages – indeed, they resist even a slowdown in the real rise – the effect of shocks in Europe has often been to throw people out of work. If companies faced by the need to adjust to changes in their marketplace and become more competitive are unable to save labour costs through more moderate pay increases, they will save labour costs through employing fewer people instead. By comparison with the United States, Europe's growth has thus been employment-lean.

There is no easy way of comparing different labour-market institutions with a simple quantitative indicator for flexibility except the end result: the unemployed as a proportion of the labour force were 10.8% in the European Union in 1997 compared with 5.2% in the United States. (A recent paper which sets out research on real wage rigidity shows that even the rank order of countries in terms of rigidity differs substantially according to the economic model chosen.)[31] Clearly, the labour market functions better in the United States. It would be wrong, however, to conclude from this comparison that Europe cannot afford to indulge in the luxury of monetary union. Unemployment is high in Europe partly because the business cycle is lagging behind the United States. There was some fall in unemployment in continental Europe during 1998 as growth rates of more than 3% exceeded those in the United States.

However, the main reason unemployment is higher is because of structural causes: higher unemployment benefits as a proportion of previous income; less intensive pressure on benefit claimants to search for work and accept jobs; more powerful trade unions when they do not co-ordinate their views; less ability to fire employees without compensation thereby making employers more cautious about hiring; and so on. These exist in Europe whether there is EMU or not. The existence of the devaluation option does not help, as we have discussed, because these same real wage rigidities which are held to be an impediment to EMU are also an impediment to the effectiveness of a devaluation. Labour-market rigidities, not the choice of monetary regime, are the principal cause of unemployment.

This point is borne out by a comparison of different European countries. Although it is true that the average level of unemployment in Europe is much higher than in the United States, the most striking feature of European unemployment is not its high average level but the

Table 3.3 Average unemployment rates, 1983–96

	%
Austria	3.8
Belgium	9.7
Denmark	9.9
Finland	9.1
France	10.4
Germany (West)	6.2
Ireland	15.1
Italy	7.6
Netherlands	8.4
Norway	4.2
Portugal	6.4
Spain	19.7
Sweden	4.3
Switzerland	1.8
United Kingdom	9.7
Canada	9.8
United States	6.5
Japan	2.6
Australia	8.7
New Zealand	6.8

Source: Nickell (1997), from OECD Employment Outlooks.

large differences between countries. As Professor Stephen Nickell has pointed out, European unemployment rates range from 1.8% in Switzerland to 19.7% in Spain if the post-recession period of 1983–96 is taken as a whole.[32] (This long period provides some guarantee against a distortion owing to different business cycle timings.) Unemployment was lower in Austria, Germany, Norway, Sweden and

Switzerland than it was in the United States.[33] In fact, nearly one-third of developed Europe's population enjoyed average unemployment rates lower than those in the United States.

Professor Nickell makes another important point in the context of the debate about monetary union, which is that the conventional wisdom on labour-market rigidities is not always right. Some types of labour-market rigidities help promote an adjustment to an external shock. For example, countries where there is co-ordination between employers or employees or both may be able to react rationally to external shocks more effectively than a so-called flexible-market country. (This may be particularly effective in small countries where most of the key players can be brought together in one room.) Nickell points out that some of the European countries with the lowest unemployment rates (Austria, Switzerland, Germany, Sweden) are not known for their labour-market flexibility, whereas the more flexible Britain has had unemployment higher than half of its European neighbours.

Nickell concludes that high unemployment is associated with four principal factors: generous benefits that run on indefinitely without a stringent test of willingness to work; high unionisation and collective bargaining without co-ordination; high overall taxes impinging on labour combined with high minimum wages for young people; and poor educational standards at the bottom of the labour market. None of these are associated with the monetary regime. All are within the power of national governments to fix whether inside or outside EMU. And all will remain a problem whether inside or outside EMU.

Summary

In this chapter we have looked at the often-cited disadvantages of EMU and some other problems that are not so well known. The removal of an independent monetary, interest-rate and exchange-rate policy will certainly entail a loss of flexibility. However, we have seen that the extent to which member countries' economies differ from each other is within the bounds seen in other monetary unions, including some

European ones. The growing interdependence of the European economies also means that an independent monetary policy is becoming less useful, and we have seen that it is too optimistic to suppose that British monetary policy has always been used in a sensible and countercyclical manner. Indeed, it has itself been a source of important shocks to the economy, notably in 1974–76 and in 1979–81. Trade patterns in Britain are not much different from those in the Euroland participants so there is no reason to expect particular shocks from that source. Also Britain's dependence on variable interest rates, a weakness arising from its inflationary history, does not make its economy more likely to react to interest-rate changes than those of existing Euroland members.

Although the Stability and Growth Pact limiting deficits and debt is unnecessarily conservative, we have also seen that the present fiscal positions of Euroland members, and of Britain, are such that there is room to absorb the impact of a normal recession without breaching the guidelines. Lastly, we have seen that Europe's unemployment rates vary widely depending on national labour-market institutions and not on the monetary regime. Those countries that suffer high unemployment and rigid labour markets would have problems inside or outside EMU. Indeed, for a devaluation to work for them they need to have labour markets which will accept that pay should not chase after prices. A devaluation, through the exercise of an independent monetary policy, therefore does not help their predicament.

4 Britain's case

Monetary union is not a zero-sum game in which one country wins what another loses. It is a win-win game in which all can win, and Britain is no exception. But there are nevertheless some specific effects of EMU for Britain which may make the benefits particularly important, and which arise out of our particular attributes. This chapter looks at some of the features of the British economy which might be affected by membership of the euro. The most important is probably our success in attracting foreign direct investment (FDI), which is particularly impressive for one of the larger EU member states. Another feature is Britain's dependence on financial services, which make up 21% of GDP. These too may be expected to benefit particularly from Britain's euro membership. This chapter also deals with the claim that Britain might become liable for the pension fund liabilities of other Euroland members, and considers the important question of how Britain would manage its currency in the new world of the euro if sterling is not to join.

Foreign direct investment

Overall, the British economy has been internationalised more rapidly than others over the last 15 years. Our outflows of direct investment have been even more substantial than our inflows, leading to a positive net balance of foreign assets in the form of direct investment. (FDI is where the stake in the company is more than 10%, generally held to be the point at which the investment ceases to be merely a part of a portfolio of shares that can be bought and sold without commitment.) However, there is no necessary connection between the outflows and the inflows. Countries can have substantial outflows which are unmatched by inflows. Germany is currently a case where outflows outstrip inflows. So Britain's success in winning over foreign investors is impressive. Indeed, Britain had inward investment worth 28.5% of GDP in 1995, more than double the EU average of 13.2% of GDP.[34] As we shall see, this success has been fundamentally as a result of Britain's EU membership, and it is now threatened by the failure to participate in the euro.

These inflows of direct investment have revolutionised manufacturing, boosting investment and productivity and introducing many working practices which had been unheard of in hidebound parts of British industry. According to Department of Trade and Industry estimates, foreign investment accounts for 26% of manufacturing output, 35% of manufacturing investment and 43% of manufacturing exports. Toyota and Nissan have built big greenfield sites. BMW has bought Rover, Ford has bought Jaguar and VW has bought Rolls-Royce and Bentley. All have embarked on or promise substantial investment programmes. But the phenomenon goes well beyond the car industry and manufacturing. Sony makes televisions in Bridgend, Wales. Intel makes microchips in Scotland. McDonald's makes hamburgers everywhere. American firms account for 3,500 plants in the United Kingdom, German firms for 1,000 and Japanese firms for 225.

Britain's success in attracting FDI appears to have continued during the 1990s. Between 1990 and 1996 Britain won 23% of all the inward investment into the EU, although its GDP accounts for just 13% of the EU total. This is the most impressive performance of any of the larger EU member states, including Spain. (On a ratio of the share of FDI to the share of GDP in the EU total, Britain outperforms all the larger member states and is exceeded only by Belgium, the Netherlands and Sweden.)[35] There are two reasons for this. The first is that a steadily rising share of British inward investment is being undertaken by companies in other EU countries; the process of vertical integration of supply chains from one EU country to another, discussed in Chapter 3, is continuing. The share of inward investment into the United

Kingdom that comes from other European countries rose from less than 10% in the early 1960s to more than 30% in the 1980s and 1990s.[36]

The second is Britain's disproportionate share of FDI coming into the EU, mainly from Japanese and American companies. In 1996 we attracted 46% of the total, more than three times as much as might have been expected if FDI had been spread throughout Europe on the basis of shares in GDP. The previous year our share of American and Japanese FDI in the EU was 25.8%, or double our GDP share. (The figures bounce around because investments are often large, but the picture of disproportionate success is clear.)

Britain is seen as part of core of EU

There are many reasons for this attraction to Britain, including the use of English, the existence of a comparatively cheap labour force, and even the provision of golf courses – a distinct plus point for Japanese managers. But a crucial reason, a necessary if not sufficient condition, is that Britain is seen as part of the core of the European Union. Anything which casts doubt on that status, and this must include the decision to stay out of the launch of the European currency, is bound to foment doubts about us in the minds of some business people. Indeed, executives of various foreign investors, notably Toyota, General Motors, Daimler-Benz and Siemens, have stated the obvious (although usually hedging about their concerns as soon as press attention became unwelcome).

The most comprehensive survey of inward investors was carried out by the Centre for Economics and Business Research in 1992. It concluded that for the increasing proportion of inward investors for whom investment in Britain was as a base to supply the entire European market, Britain's participation in the euro was important in ensuring a continuing flow of investment.[37] But this is not just a matter of surveys, conjecture or anecdote; it is also the evidence of history. Before the European Union was set up by the Treaty of Rome in 1957

Britain's share of FDI into the countries of the Community was about 40%. It then declined dramatically to 15% over the period when we were outside from 1958 to 1973, and then it climbed up again.[38]

At present, most business people, including prospective foreign direct investors, believe that Britain will join the single currency. But if that perception were to change we might well begin to lose the job-building investment that has done so much to revive some of the poorest and most depressed regions of the country, including South Wales, the North-west and the North-east. More than half of the jobs created by inward direct investment have gone to these comparatively poor areas, and foreign investment has been largely responsible for their regeneration and diversification away from declining industries such as textiles, shipbuilding and coal. If we fail to join the euro we will lose one of the most important motors of prosperity of the last 20 years.

Financial services

Apart from Britain's prowess in attracting FDI, the other peculiarity of the British economy which may be affected by EMU is financial services, particularly the wholesale markets centred on the City of London. Britain already has a high share of GDP coming from the FIREB (finance, insurance, real estate and business services) industries, which reflects the early liberalisation of this sector during the 1980s together with the diminution of state support for earnings in retirement. As a result Britain's institutional investors (insurers and pension funds) control the third largest amount of money under management of any economy in the world. The focus of this subsector of the financial industry is the equity and bond markets centred on London. Indeed, London and the South-east region are particularly dependent on the high-growth, high-income financial sector, together accounting for half of the United Kingdom's GDP generated in financial services.[39]

The City has become a magnet for foreign financial firms, and the rest of the European Union has made a significant contribution to the influx. According to a recent study by the Centre for Economic and

Business Research, the number of EU-based banks with subsidiaries or branches in the City grew from 100 in 1975 to 241 in 1997, and just over half are full subsidiaries employing 22,800 staff.[40] The 24 German banks in London now employ 8,800 people and the 18 French banks employ 5,800. Several big continental banks, notably Deutsche Bank and Union Bank of Switzerland, are focusing their investment banking operations on London rather than Frankfurt or Zürich.

London banks service much of EU

These institutions are involved in international business of all sorts, but banks in London are increasingly servicing an EU-wide hinterland. Overall, a recent study for the Corporation of London shows that the proportion of City turnover originating in other EU member states is now 16.5%. The share is highest for international banking, where it is 37%. The proportion is also high in corporate finance (that is, advice on funding for companies), equities, derivatives, foreign exchange and professional services.[41] The study estimates that about 41,000 jobs out of a City total of 250,000 are dependent on the rest of the EU. Fortunately, little of this business is associated with exchange-rate transactions between European currencies that are about to disappear. Less than one-fifth of foreign-exchange trading involving Deutschemarks also involves other Euroland currencies.

The conventional wisdom is that the City will continue to be the dominant financial centre in the European time zone whether Britain joins the euro or not. There are powerful effects at work. Once a business has sunk investment into an area it is reluctant to move. The fact that so much business is done in the City means that there is an incentive to do even more business there, because of easy access to investors, investment bankers, legal advisers, accountants, insurers and all the other infrastructure which grows up whenever people intensively practise a particular trade. Moreover, it is part of the City's own folklore that it only became an international financial centre again at the end of the 1960s because of heavy-handed regulation in New York. The burden of banking and financial market supervision on Wall Street made London a more attractive place to deposit and lend dollars, and the eurodollar market was born. A number of City people believe that any similar attempt to over-regulate the euro area could redound to the City's advantage.

There is, though, a certain amount of whistling to keep your spirits up in this sort of attitude. If Britain were to stay out of the euro area there would certainly be no dramatic effects on London unless the government were to score some own goal such as agreeing a with-holding tax on interest. (This is not impossible. Although the British government has a veto on tax matters, the Major government agreed a VAT rate on art dealing which had the effect of exporting much of London's art business to New York and Geneva.) But it seems at least likely that London would be unable to capitalise on the opportunity to become Europe's financial centre, or to become what New York is to the United States. This could be a substantial missed opportunity. We have already discussed, in Chapter 2, the likely development of inte-grated European capital markets as investors are able to shop for the best buys across the whole euro area without taking exchange-rate risks. Given the advantages of critical mass in financial markets, it is likely that these markets will gradually converge on one centre.

EU funds management is a growing area

If we look at the areas where EU business is least significant for London the management of EU funds comes lowest.[42] This is partly because there are fewer institutional funds to manage in France and Germany, which together account for about $2.2 trillion compared with $1.7 trillion under management in Britain.[43] But this will change over the next ten years as both countries move away from state provision for retirement and the trend that has already been observed in Britain and the United States sets in. Given the size of the French and German economies, and the high savings rates, their institutional funds are likely to overtake those available in Britain fairly rapidly as soon as pension reform gets under way. If Britain is outside the euro area it seems inherently less plausible that it will be able to enjoy the lion's share of domestically generated business.

After all, the focus of the euro money markets will be in Frankfurt, which is where the decisions on interest rates will be taken. This will therefore also become the focus for the bond market, as judgments on short-term policy interest rates crucially affect the perception of longer-term, fixed-interest securities. The idea that Frankfurt will be as insignificant as Washington, the headquarters of the US Federal Reserve, overlooks the fact that Frankfurt already has substantial financial markets whereas Washington has none. No other monetary area has ever seen its principal financial markets grow up in a country outside the jurisdiction of its banking supervisors, and it is hard to imagine that the Euroland policymakers would be happy to see this happen if Britain did not participate.

The euro participants have already been reluctant to allow London-based banks to participate fully in TARGET, a settlement system for euro financial institutions, the speed of which will give them a natural advantage in euro business. Moreover, the continent's financial exchanges have shown their ability to win substantial volumes back from London. The Deutsche Terminboerse (DTB), Frankfurt's stock exchange, slashed the costs of trading futures contracts in German bunds (government bonds) and won the volume back from the London International Financial Futures Exchange (LIFFE). The London Stock Exchange seems to have recognised the threat to its position by agreeing to set up a joint venture with the DTB in which, despite London's vastly greater market value, the German exchange will have a 50% stake. Another straw in the wind was the decision in the summer of 1998 of GEC and Alsthom to float their own joint venture, Alstom, on the Paris bourse so that its principal quotation would be in euros.

Nor should the City or British policymakers rely on a level playing field. The financial authorities in France, in particular, take a thoroughly interventionist view about promoting Paris as a financial centre. When the City began to trade the majority of deals in French government bonds in the late 1980s the then head of the French Trésor, Jean-Claude Trichet, launched a fierce campaign to repatriate the bond market to Paris. The securities were streamlined to make them easier to buy and sell. The Trésor also conducted a major marketing campaign, and it is reputed to have put the word around the French banks that it would take a dim view if they continued to trade in bulk through London. Within months the market had shifted back to Paris. In the light of such experiences there has to be a risk that the French authorities might see it to their advantage to keep Britain out of the euro area for as long as possible, rather as General de Gaulle kept Britain out of the European Community. It would not be hard to engineer a pretext to do so; insistence on two years for sterling within a revamped ERM would prove extremely difficult to sell in Britain.

In conclusion, the City has great strengths which will not be eroded quickly. Both Frankfurt and Paris are small financial centres by comparison; as British officials point out, there are more people merely employed in financial services in London than live in Frankfurt. But a decision to stay out of the euro area for any length of time would undoubtedly chip away at London's dominance, and would increasingly lead to missed opportunities as the Euroland markets developed elsewhere. Much of the talk on this subject misses the point. The threat to London's role as an offshore international centre is perhaps less significant than the opportunity to develop London as the true financial centre for its continent, in the same way as New York is the key financial centre for the United States.

Do the real opportunities lie elsewhere?

Against these points some Eurosceptics argue that there is no point in integrating Britain even further into Europe because the real opportunities lie elsewhere in the high-growth markets around the world.

Until the onset of the Asian regional crisis, with the devaluation of the Thai baht in July 1997, a favourite candidate for the Eurosceptics was the high-growth economies of Asia-Pacific.[44] These economies do have real strengths which will ensure that they recover before long and resume their growth. But the idea that we should ignore Europe, even though it has traditionally been more slow-growing than the Asian economies, is absurd.

The rest of the European Union takes about 54% of our total exports of goods and services, whereas all developing economies put together, not just Asia-Pacific but Latin America and the oil-producing economies as well, take just 16.4%.[45] Simple arithmetic shows that the growth rate of exports to the developing world would have to be three times the growth rate of exports to the European Union to provide the same absolute increase in sales and jobs. Moreover, the argument that Britain should either integrate with Europe or pursue opportunities in Asia is fundamentally flawed. In truth, we can and should do both. The more successful we are in the European single market, the more attractive our products are likely to be in world markets outside. If we do well in Europe we will do better in Asia. Economics is not a zero-sum game.

Unfunded pension liabilities

Another common Eurosceptic misconception is that somehow Britain, if it were to join the single European currency, would ultimately become liable for vast hidden liabilities incurred by other European countries. The most compelling candidate in this saga is the so-called unfunded pension liabilities, the extent to which countries are not raising enough in taxation or social-security obligations to meet the promises that they have made to future pensioners. Various estimates of these unfunded liabilities have been made. One of the more authoritative was done recently by the IMF and suggests that Britain's unfunded liabilities amount to just 19% of GDP, compared with 98% of GDP in France, 113% in Italy and 139% in Germany.[46]

It is important to be clear what these calculations are. They project the future pensioner population, and then they project what those pensioners will be paid, over and above what will be coming into the exchequer in contributions, if present pension policies remain in place. Lastly, they work out the sum of money that would be necessary for a government to invest now if it were to pay all those extra unfunded pensions out of its investment. (For the more financially sophisticated, the calculation is of the net present value of all future pension liabilities minus the net present value of future contributions.)

Whatever else this calculation is, it is not the calculation of a debt. There is no contractual obligation on the part of governments to fund pensions at present levels forever, and we now have many examples of governments which have reformed their pension systems precisely to diminish or abolish this problem. Indeed, Britain used to have an enormous unfunded pension liability because the state pension used to rise in line with earnings and there was a state earnings-related pension supplement (SERPS). Margaret Thatcher cut this unfunded liability in one fell swoop by linking the basic future old-age pension to prices rather than earnings and by curbing SERPS. The Italian government has already made a start on tackling its own unfunded liabilities, and the German and French governments are widely expected to do so. The most admired model touted as an alternative to these expensive state schemes is the Chilean system, which involves mandatory contributions to personal pension funds invested by fund managers over which the saver has discretion.

The point about these so-called unfunded liabilities is that they are not a debt but an analytical tool for telling us that pensions policy is unsustainable. Another way of expressing the same concept is to look at the tax and contribution rate which would be necessary to fund the rise in pensions dictated by present policies and the demographic trends of an ageing population. It is almost the definition of the state's role in the economy that it should take on commitments which involve too much uncertainty for the private sector. But we do not look at the unfunded liability involved in educating all future generations of school children, or of defending the realm, or of providing health care. But if we were to perform the same calculation for the National Health Service – working out the sum of money needed to ensure that its present spending growth could continue forever – we would find a huge unfunded liability. But we do not do any such calculation. So it is important not to become overawed by these apparently large numbers or to confuse them with real and much more contractually enforceable debts.

The world will change

There is a final point about the specific nature of Britain's case which the Eurosceptics overlook. They assume that Britain can opt for a world which remains broadly unchanged from the one that we are in today, despite the creation of the euro. In fact, the existence of such a large currency, encompassing 11 economies with a combined GDP only a little short of that of the United States, is likely to complicate British monetary policy if we remain outside.

As we have seen, nearly half of Britain's trade is with the 11 members of Euroland. Imports from Euroland account for 46% of all imports, and therefore nearly half of the inflationary impact of any rise or fall in the pound will originate with Euroland and the euro. This is nearly four times as much as the importance to inflation of American imports. But it is also true that short-term capital flows move the pound up and down in line with the dollar. So we may find the pound moving sharply with the dollar and making life extremely bumpy for all those who depend on continental markets. Moreover, the volatility of the exchange rate between the euro and the dollar is likely to be much greater than it is at present, because the European Central Bank is likely to care much less about movements in the external value of the currency as imports will be a comparatively small share of the euro area. Euroland's exports will account for just 11% of GDP, only a little more than exports in the United States or Japan. The euro area will become a continent-wide marketplace of a similar size to the United States, and its policymakers are likely to be just as unworried about movements in its exchange rate.[47]

It could therefore be hard for the neighbours of the euro to hang on to its coat-tails, even though it will be more important for their own inflation and trade competitiveness that they do. Like it or not, the British economy will be more intimately dependent on Euroland and its currency than any other area. As a result British policymakers' tolerance of sharp movements against the euro is likely to be low. Combined with the probability that the euro will be volatile against the dollar, British interest rates may have to move rapidly up and down to reduce the movement of the pound against the euro. Join it or not, the euro will be too big to ignore.

Summary

This chapter has looked at the special importance of the euro for the maintenance of Britain's good record on FDI and the position of financial services within the economy. In both cases there are sound reasons for believing that a decision to adopt the euro will benefit Britain, whereas a decision to stay out will increasingly endanger these traditional advantages. It also examined the argument that Britain would have to assume the unfunded pension liabilities of other euro participants, and pointed out how different these so called liabilities are from normal debt. In addition, the Maastricht Treaty prohibits any bail-out of one government by others. Lastly, it considered the increased difficulties British policymakers are likely to face if we do not join as a result of our intimate dependence on Euroland and the euro.

5 The political consequences of EMU

In this chapter we look first at James Forder's fear that we would be delegating extraordinary powers to unelected officials if we were to join the euro. We then turn to the fear that the euro is merely a stalking horse for a much wider and deeper process of European integration. In effect, the euro is, in this view, a step towards a European superstate. Lastly, we look at some more likely results from the creation of the euro and the new realpolitik of a Europe largely controlled by centre-left governments in Britain, France, Germany and Italy for the first time since the second world war.

Delegating powers to unelected officials

Part of the political compromise that created the euro was that the European Central Bank (ECB) should be modelled largely on the German Bundesbank, a central bank which has a track record second to none of controlling inflation during the post-war period. An essential element of the ECB's credibility with the financial markets is that it inherits the Bundesbank's mantle. It will be independent of political pressures to set interest rates, and will therefore deliver low and stable inflation. This is why investors are prepared to lend money to governments participating in the euro at substantially lower interest rates (1 percentage point at the time of writing) than they are to Britain.

Will we, though, be selling our democratic heritage for a mess of pottage? If so, it is surprising how many other countries have done this already, both inside and outside the group of euro participants. Indeed, Britain was the last country of the Group of Seven leading industrial economies to make its central bank independent when Gordon Brown, the chancellor of the exchequer, adopted Liberal Democrat policy after the general election of 1997. Do we really believe that France, Germany, Italy, Canada, Japan or the United States were less democratic than Britain because they delegated powers to a specialised institution? Do we really think that Britain became fundamentally less democratic when Mr Brown handed the setting of interest rates to the Bank of England's Monetary Policy Committee? And what about the situation in Britain before 1946, when the Bank of England was nationalised? Were we less democratic then?

Our politicians have delegated many powers to institutions at one remove from political temptation, including the Arts Council, the British Broadcasting Corporation, National Health Service trusts, the Mersey Docks and Harbour Board, regional development authorities, the Docklands Development Corporation, and so on. The ECB is not different. Experience suggests that monetary policy is better conducted by people who do not have a direct interest in using it to secure their own re-election. Having an institution that is thoroughly credible in its anti-inflationary credentials may mean that governments regain some power to use fiscal policy (taxation and spending) to cushion movements in their economies within the limits of the Maastricht Treaty. The lack of credibility of most European governments since their reactions to the 1973–74 and 1979–80 oil-price shocks has taken years to put right.

Indeed, it was precisely the inability of most politicians to respond rapidly to the need for higher interest rates in the early 1970s that created many of the problems in Europe today. Politicians were intrinsically too inclined to take the soft option with the result that inflation got out of hand, and the ultimate measures taken to control it were far more draconian and damaging to the economy than if a stitch had been taken in time. It is therefore perfectly possible to support central bank independence without believing in monetarism, despite James Forder's arguments, because experience shows that politically controlled interest rates are too slow to go up and too quick to come down. Independent central banks are simply designed to ensure that the stitch in time saves nine.

People who now argue that politicians should be given back control over interest rates appear to have forgotten the sad circumstances which led most informed people to conclude that politicians should not control interest rates. In Britain another classic example was the failure of Kenneth Clarke, the Conservative chancellor of the exchequer, to raise interest rates in the run-up to the 1997 general election. Yet there are few economists who would argue that he was right. He was simply putting his party's electoral interest ahead of the interest in longer-term economic management.

Three models of central banking

Within the overall group of independent central banks there are three broad models. In the United States the Federal Reserve Board (Fed) is unique in that it is meant explicitly to take account of jobs as well as inflation. In Britain and New Zealand the central banks are meant to look only at inflation, but the government sets the target for them to aim at. In other central banks, including all the continental European banks and now the ECB, the central bank itself is enjoined to aim at price stability. In the case of the ECB it has defined this as a range of inflation of 0–2%.

There is much less to choose between these arrangements than some suggest because paper constitutions are only one influence on actual decisions. People matter, and so does the social environment. The Bundesbank has always been acutely aware of its political support in the country as any central bank must be. It has been able to take tough decisions because of the German folk memory of hyperinflation under the Weimar republic in the 1920s. This has certainly been of much more importance to the Bundesbank than its 'monetarism' as it repeatedly missed its monetary targets. That history of hyperinflation will be less of a consideration for the ECB because few other countries shared the experience. Indeed, if the ECB were seen to be acting in an irresponsibly restrictive manner, driving inflation down too far and too fast, it would soon have to respond to the arguments and pressures from business and the trade unions.

At the other end of the spectrum, the Fed should perhaps have been more relaxed than other central banks both because it is meant to consider the employment effects of its policies and because the United States has never suffered a hyperinflation like Germany. But under Paul Volcker, the Fed pursued a tighter monetary policy against inflation in 1979 than almost any other central bank. So, once again, the paper constitution matters less than the people making the decisions and the context in which they work. There will, of course, always be doves and hawks. In the case of the ECB, its president, Wim Duisenberg, is a former Social Democratic finance minister, although he is widely perceived as a hawk. However, the hawks (including Hans Tietmeyer of the Bundesbank and Jean-Claude Trichet now of the Banque de France) have already been outvoted on some provisions of the new institution.

Far from being rigidly monetarist, the new ECB has adopted monetary policy guidelines which many commentators have found surprisingly pragmatic. There will be no formal money supply targets because of the difficulties of knowing what a particular measure of the money supply may mean. So the ECB will not begin life even formally as a monetarist institution. It will take into account a wide range of indicators, including the exchange rate, money supply and inflation itself, when aiming for its 0–2% range. The ECB will give regular evidence to the European Parliament on its policies and progress, and the parliament will no doubt have a considerable incentive to ensure that the ECB is more open than it has been until now about its policies and thinking.

Shifts in the political climate
This is part of the answer to the concern that Europe will now be in thrall to the super-restrictive prejudices of the ECB. Another part is the shift in the political climate within Europe, where all four of the biggest member states of the European Union are now controlled by

centre-left governments. If part of Europe's problem is indeed lack of sufficient spending power, that part may well be put right more quickly than many think. The Euro-11 council of ministers (comprising the finance ministers of the countries that are participating in the euro) is clearly determined to create a political counterweight to the ECB, and some of the leading members are thinking of packages to keep demand going despite the Asian crisis. Indeed, the balance within the ECB is likely to tilt even further in a pragmatic direction when Mr Tietmeyer's term expires in August 1999. The new Social Democrat finance minister and a leading left-winger in his party, Oskar Lafontaine, will play a key role in the German chancellor's choice of his successor.

With luck, Europe will be able to strike a new and healthy balance between an ECB which continues to have anti-inflationary credibility (and can therefore ensure low long-term borrowing costs and low price rises) and a political dimension which can tackle unemployment through both fiscal boosts to spending power and measures to deal with structural unemployment. Any fiscal packages will have much more effect if they are co-ordinated, because the increase in spending power in one country rapidly creates demand for goods and services in others. Indeed, the segmentation of Europe into national currency areas, and the resulting fear of exchange-rate crises if economic policy became too expansionary, was probably a significant factor behind Europe's poor performance in the 1970s and 1980s. The euro, together with the election of Lionel Jospin in France and Gerhard Schröder in Germany, has changed the game and may make fears of excessively tight policies look curiously old-fashioned. Like generals, economists are too prone to fight the last war.

A cover for political union?

There is a second strand of concern about the euro, which is that it is a plot to drag us into a political union. Certainly, there are many people in Europe who actively want the process of integration to continue and deepen and for whom EMU is an important step. They hope that a single currency will provide a spur to a common foreign and defence policy and maybe other common policies too. But they are not necessarily right. Whether the single currency entails further political consequences will be a matter for decision in an intergovernmental conference at some point in the future. When those decisions come to be made, Britain will have the absolute right to veto changes because any treaty amendment has to be ratified by each country. So in legal and constitutional terms it is incorrect to say that Maastricht will entail further integration. Indeed, the hopes of the German government, among others, that a single currency would spur a substantial development of political union were dashed, despite the commitment to an intergovernmental conference which led to the revisions in the Treaty of Amsterdam. There was no substantial extension of majority voting, even though there was a general recognition that a Union with 21 rather than 15 members cannot allow itself to be held hostage by one state.

The single currency may, of course, eventually set up political processes which will lead to these constitutional changes. If the single currency is perceived to be a great success, providing all the benefits outlined in Chapter 2 and more, much of the existing scepticism about European institutions may begin to erode. There may be more willingness to embark upon EU decision processes in other areas which are currently up to intergovernmental co-operation (such as foreign affairs and defence). The governments of Britain, France and Germany have already told their defence industries to bring forward plans for integration, which would allow them to compete with the newly consolidated American defence resulting from the mergers of Lockheed and Martin Marietta (now Lockheed Martin) and of Boeing and McDonnell Douglas (Boeing). Arguably, this is being determined by defence economics. The existing national defence orders and companies are simply too small to make the production runs big enough to contain the ever-spiralling costs of high-technology weaponry. Once the defence procurement and defence industries of Britain, France and Germany are integrated, the ability to wage independent warfare will become even more circumscribed. A further integration of the forces themselves will seem only a short step; strategic defence reviews will increasingly take account not of national but of joint capabilities.

A successful monetary union may hasten integration in other areas by providing evidence of what can be done at European level. But the Eurosceptics do not generally argue that we should stay out of EMU because it will be successful. They say instead that EMU will fail. And if it fails in some spectacular manner there is little doubt that the debacle would cast a pall over all the European Union's institutions and would create serious doubts about the advisability of further integration. Far from hastening a European superstate, EMU would then have driven a nail into its coffin.

Many economists in the financial sector and academe have tried hard to envisage circumstances in which EMU might break up.[48] One scenario is an Italian political and financial crisis which leads to the wholesale flight of Italian money into German bank accounts and banknotes (ahead of the time when the euro becomes a physical reality in 2002), and which causes the Germans to reintroduce a separate monetary policy for fear of contagion. Given the large amount of short-term debt issued by Italy and Belgium (a short maturity which means that investors have to continue to make decisions to renew their investment, and which is therefore vulnerable to a shift in sentiment), this is not an outlandish prospect.

Nevertheless, these sorts of scenarios have generally lacked credibility with the financial markets. All three leading credit-rating agencies regard the chances of such a break-up as small enough to warrant awarding the monetary union the coveted AAA status. The markets themselves increasingly price government securities of the euro members in line with differences in their debt and fiscal performance, ignoring currency and inflation-risk differences.

Maastricht plan may need amendment

A more tangible risk, which might have political consequences, is that the Maastricht architecture may need amendment because it is deemed to be inadequate. If EMU proves to create difficulties for some or several member states there will almost certainly be pressure for changes in procedures, and these could involve greater integration. The Treaty itself was the outcome of a laborious process of negotiation, which included many compromises, and in certain key respects it is already out of date. For example, it insists on a set of convergence criteria, including exchange-rate stability within the ERM, which looked sensible before the ERM crisis of 1992–93 but which now looks odd. We know that markets can attack currencies even if their fundamentals are strong and there is no need for devaluation – look at the attack on the French franc in 1993. It is precisely because of the difficulty of sustaining a fixed exchange rate in a world of free capital flows that the case for a single currency becomes even more compelling.

The most likely candidate for causing trouble is the Stability and Growth Pact (SGP) and the commitments in the Treaty itself to low deficits. These restrictions were introduced at German insistence to limit the possibility that large government deficits and debts might eventually set up a strong incentive for the monetary authorities to lend a member government money, and hence increase the money supply and inflation. The processes will certainly address this risk of political incontinence most effectively, but with the danger of introducing unnecessary limitations on the freedom of action of member states. These restrictions inevitably hamper a member state's ability to use fiscal policy to stabilise its own economy if it is faced by a particular shock. Under the SGP a country has to seek the approval of the Council of Ministers if it is likely to run a deficit of more than 3% of GDP unless GDP itself is falling by 2% in that year. This rigidity may in turn mean that there will be greater pressure to deal with such shocks at a Europe-wide level rather than at the national level.[49] Ironically, Germany's insistence on measures designed to protect it from other countries' profligacy may entail new fiscal measures overall.

Of course, if a country has already steered its deficit to within the limits that would normally allow it to weather a recession without breaching the 3% guideline, this is unlikely to be a large problem. But it is hard to see why a country with a low level of debt should not, if it wants, react to a particularly grave recession with an even more active fiscal policy, such as bringing forward infrastructure spending and cutting taxes. In other circumstances a country may have a large public capital programme to improve infrastructure, which might put in place assets counterbalancing any increased deficit. Yet the Maastricht Treaty prohibits even a country which has paid off all its national debt from running budget deficits of more than 3% of GDP each year without the approval of the Council of Ministers. A sensible change would therefore be to allow governments with debt well within the 60% of GDP limit to have greater flexibility to use fiscal policy as they see fit, and leave the markets to decide what the cost of funds should be. If a government is seen to have embarked on an irresponsible policy it will certainly pay a price in a high cost of funds when it borrows.

There is another reason for supposing that the SGP may have to made more flexible: the ageing of the population. If governments are to shift their liabilities for pensions on to funded personal saving schemes, they will need to divert some of the existing contributions paid to government into mandatory personal pension contributions. But this shift to a funded scheme inevitably involves a period when the government is paying for the pensions of the existing pensioners but is going without the contributions of future pensioners. Those future pensioners would be paying that money into a funded scheme. There would therefore be some temporary worsening in the government's budget deficit even though the longer-term solvency of the government is improving, in that it is reducing a potential liability. It would be odd to penalise countries for making such a move, since it is an essential part of making their pension schemes sustainable for the future. Moreover, there are no effects in stoking up demand from such an increase in the budget deficit, which is a purely financial transaction. People make contributions to their personal funds rather than to the government. The overall level of national savings remains the same.

Member states may develop their own solutions
It is also possible that member states may develop other means of absorbing shocks to their economy which will help to stabilise the Europe-wide economy. The use of fiscal policy (taxation and public spending) was originally advocated by John Maynard Keynes as a way of encouraging more spending by consumers and businesses. But it may be possible to develop levers which have similar effects, and which bypass the fiscal process. For example, many European countries are now actively considering reforms of their old-age pension provision which would involve mandatory contributions to a personal retire-ment fund, in effect, compulsory savings. Most already have fiscal incentives for employees to save for their retirement. It would be a simple matter to ask a council of economic advisers to vary both the compulsory contributions and the incentives in line with the business cycle in each country. There would be higher contributions in booms when saving needs to be encouraged and lower ones in recessions when spending is in order. Such countercyclical measures would lack the political difficulties traditionally associated with the active use of fiscal policy, when higher public spending undertaken in slow years continues into fast ones, ratcheting up the scale of government. (This idea was adopted as Liberal Democrat policy in the autumn of 1998 as part of a series of proposals to prepare Britain for membership of EMU.)

Another interesting idea, put forward by Giles Keating of CS First Boston, an investment bank, is that countries might vary the capital requirements of their banks depending on the state of the business cycle. Capital, mainly shareholders' funds, is the cushion that banks have to use to pay depositors if loans turn bad. At present, banks have to keep a minimum amount of capital worth 8% of their lending and other assets (such as government bonds). If there were a particularly strong upswing under way which affected the prices of assets, such as property and shares, banks would have to have more of their own shareholders' funds to back a given amount of lending. This would recognise the increased future risks of such lending. But it would also make such lending less attractive to the bank, giving policymakers another lever to influence overall spending in the economy. If there were a recession such capital adequacy ratios would be allowed to decline, enabling more lending for a given amount of capital. Since banking regulation remains a national responsibility within EMU, this could be introduced by any participating member.

What if such flexibility, faced with a shock for a particular member country, were not enough? Eurosceptics worry that EMU may need a much more substantial degree of support at the federal level to make it sustainable. After all, the federal level of government in most federal states spends some 20–25% of GDP, whereas the European Union budget is less than 2% of GDP. As we have seen, much of the spending which would normally be undertaken by a federation is currently undertaken at national level in Europe. However, the often high spending by the central government in federations entails a surprisingly small amount of genuine insurance of one state by the federation. I have already cited the evidence that shows that the American system insures only about 10 cents in every dollar fall in state income, rather than the 30 cents that some studies have suggested.[50] The study goes on to show that a fairly small amount of 'fiscal federalism' (a fiscal system at supranational level) might be necessary to achieve such a result provided that it was clearly targeted as an insurance system, rather than merely the side effect of providing many other public goods and services (such as, in the United States, the postal service and Medicare). However, it also shows that it might be difficult for the member states to reach agreement on such a system since the states with more volatile economies would have a greater interest in the proposal than those with more stable ones.

This general conclusion – that there does not need to be a substantial amount of EU-level spending – is in line with a major study on the same subject done for the European Commission, which was the product of a panel under the chairmanship of Sir Donald MacDougall.[51] The MacDougall committee, in line with the spirit of the times (1977) in which it reported, stressed the importance of having a constant redistribution from rich to poor regions rather than merely insuring against sudden shifts. Its scope therefore went well beyond what has been regarded as politically saleable in recent times. But even MacDougall concluded that, in order to achieve a redistributive effect of some 40% of regional inequalities (in line with the effect of national budgets), the EU budget would need to rise to something of the order of 2–7% of GDP (7.5–10% of GDP if defence were included). In other words, a careful targeting of Community policies would leave the EU-wide level of government at only one-third the size of the federal levels of governments in Germany, Canada or the United States.[52] Moreover, MacDougall was careful to propose programmes which could more effectively be undertaken at European level, so that there would be no overall addition to general government spending.

These studies are important because they must allay the fears of many Europeans that a superstate in Brussels will be a consequence of the single currency. It is possible – indeed, it is likely – that the existing framework of Maastricht will be adequate to the challenges it will face. Its inflexibilities might be dealt with by the development of new policy levers, or by the further delegation of powers to the national governments over fiscal policy. This is by no means impossible. The Maastricht architecture is not written in stone and will certainly continue to develop. Moreover, the fiscal provisions should be easy to change, since the key provisions of the SGP form part of a Council regulation rather than the Treaty itself and can therefore be changed by the Council of Ministers.

But even if this route is not chosen, and some EU-wide insurance system or even a permanently redistributive system as proposed by

MacDougall is deemed necessary, the size of the EU budget would remain small as a proportion of income by comparison with the size of national member states' budgets. The European Union is, it is true, already an incipient federation, but it will always remain unique and is unlikely to follow the same path as other federations. The national government level will remain far, far stronger, even if the Maastricht architecture has to be amended as radically as the most pessimistic fear. Therefore there is no ratchet to a centralised superstate. Given some of the misconceptions about Maastricht, it is also worth pointing out that the Treaty's limits apply only to deficits and debt and do not affect a country's ability to fund whatever level of public spending it sees fit through taxation, depending on its national and ideological preferences.

International political consequences

Turning to international consequences, much will depend on the development of the euro as a reserve currency used by central banks to intervene in setting their own currency's level. The more important the euro becomes as an international asset, the greater the call will be for a collective European view. At present, the European role in helping to resolve crises, such as the Mexican currency crash in December 1994 or the Asian crisis in the wake of the Thai baht devaluation in July 1997, is minimal. Several European governments, particularly the German government, were riled that the US Treasury unilaterally decided on the Mexican rescue package with minimal prior consultation. In Asia the Europeans have been bit players. But Europe would certainly be expected to play a far more significant role if the euro internationalises quickly, a process that is likely to be hastened still further by British membership. This in turn will put pressure on the Euroland finance ministers to come to common positions on many of the big financial issues of the day. Indeed, this could be essential for financial stability. If the dollar's role is seriously weakened, the United States will be correspondingly less able to lead from the front in resolving financial crises.

Britain's membership of the euro would be likely to have another political consequence, as it would strengthen the more liberal and market-oriented forces within the group. Each participating member has, of course, both market-oriented and interventionist or dirigiste political forces. But, in general, the commitment to free trade, free capital flows and the exercise of restraint in any government intervention has been strongest in the northern countries: Austria, Britain, Denmark, Germany, Ireland, the Netherlands and Sweden. British membership, which would probably be accompanied soon after by Danish and Swedish membership, would tilt the balance decisively. The practical consequences would be felt across a wide range of issues, including the burden of regulation imposed on the banking system and the extent of residual national controls. Indeed, Britain's exclusion from the first wave of entrants may already have had an influence by default on the ECB's operating procedures, notably the insistence on a mandatory cash-reserve requirement for banks and the extremely conservative pronouncements on what the ECB will publish. The president has confirmed the generally unhelpful tone of the ECB's dealings with its interlocutors in the markets and elsewhere by suggesting that the minutes of committees, in contrast to both the British and the American practice of publication with six weeks' delay, should be subject to a 16-year publication delay.

6 **Options and conclusions**

The British, by temperament, prefer small and gradual changes. Over time these changes may build up, but there should be nothing too dramatic or revolutionary if we can help it. EMU is therefore everything that British policymakers usually dislike. It is a large, dramatic, discontinuous and radical change. Indeed, it is the largest change in international monetary arrangements since the Bretton Woods system after the second world war. It is arguably the largest single change in the framework of economic policy that has ever been tried in Europe, including Bretton Woods and the gold standard. It is, by its nature, a leap of faith.

Many of its elements and its characteristics are surrounded by uncertainty. This is one reason there are so many different economic views on monetary union. Economists are usually good at coming to agreed answers on limited questions such as 'What will happen to consumer spending if incomes go up?' They are less good at answering conclusively questions such as 'Should we join a monetary union?' when there are so many different factors to weigh in the balance, and when it is possible for reasonable people to attribute a different weight to differing costs and benefits.

What is, however, incontrovertible is that monetary union has happened, and it has happened on a much larger scale than most British policymakers, let alone the Eurosceptics, ever believed possible. With 11 founding members, Euroland is a currency area of similar size to the United States, with a similar weight on the world economic stage. This fundamentally alters the status quo. Until January 1st 1999, the pound was just another European currency among many. But now it is a comparatively small currency set against a vast one, the movements of which completely dominate the inflationary impact of import prices and the competitiveness of British exporters. The potential for great volatility in sterling has increased, particularly since the relationship between the euro and the dollar is itself likely to be more volatile as their respective monetary authorities care little about their exchange rates (since they affect only a small part of their now continent-wide economies).

In this context Britain cannot merely opt out and pretend that nothing is happening. If we are to stay out of the euro we must expect an even bumpier ride than we have had over the last 25 years of a largely floating exchange rate for sterling. We will need to reinforce the credibility of our monetary institutions, which will otherwise bear unfavourable comparison with those of the United States and Euroland.[53] We will also have to ensure that fiscal policy remains on track, as the cost of market punishment will be greater outside the euro than inside it. Not only can bond yields rise if the markets disapprove of a government's policy, but the exchange rate can fall. Moreover, the exchange rate may well come under strain because of developments in either the United States or Euroland and require offsetting fiscal and interest-rate changes to compensate. After all, the Deutschemark/pound exchange rate was DM2.95 during our membership of the ERM from 1990 to 1992, when it fell to less than DM2.4. It rose to DM2.6 in 1994, dropping to just DM2.2 in 1995 before beginning a strong uptrend again in 1996 and recovering the old central parity in the ERM in June 1997. With the euro the rate could be every bit as volatile, but more than half our exports will be going to the area. In other words, the counterfactual 'what would happen if we don't go in' does not look attractive.

The balance of costs and benefits points to British entry. The costs are often overstated. The divergences that have in the past occurred among the European economies – the problem that a one-size-fits-all monetary policy is meant to aggravate – have already been experienced in other monetary unions, notably the United States but also existing

European countries. An independent monetary policy (both interest rates and exchange rate) is a diminishing asset in a world which is becoming increasingly interdependent. Moreover, it is wrong to assume that the freedoms an independent policy affords are unalloyed benefits. Many of the greatest shocks administered to the British economy over the post-war period have been home-grown instances of ill-judged policy, including far greater and more sudden shocks to our trading sectors (such as manufacturing in 1979–81) than are imaginable in EMU. The lack of an independent exchange rate and interest rate will put pressure on the remaining means of adjustment – the labour market – but this is already more flexible than it was, and Britain is certainly as well able to adjust as other large EMU participants. We have also seen that Britain's economy is not disproportionately affected by short-term interest rates, despite the importance of variable-rate mortgages.

On the benefits side, the euro will improve growth and jobs by two principal means: it will increase efficiency and reduce risks. Consumers will have more choice and greater ease in comparing prices. Competitive pressures will increase and so will efficiency. This is perhaps the most fundamental step forward, albeit often underestimated by our macroeconomically obsessed policymakers. It will make a reality of the single European market and provide businesses with opportunities for economies of scale of which they can at present only dream. The single market will increase prospective returns on investment, and thereby growth and jobs. There will also be an elimination of the transactions costs in moving from the pound to the euro.

The second mechanism by which EMU delivers important benefits is through the reduction of risks, particularly exchange-rate uncertainty. This may be expected to boost trade flows, but, even more crucially, it should also boost investment across borders within EMU and raise the long-run growth rate of the European Union. By creating a monetary area that is a continent-wide economy, EMU also insulates its member economies from external shocks caused either by problems in other economies or by financial flows and misaligned exchange rates. It lifts the constraint which British policymakers have often felt: the need to ensure that the balance of payments (of exports and imports) does not go too far into deficit. Within EMU the balance of payments can no longer have a traumatic effect on the exchange rate of an individual member state, or on its inflation rate.

EMU also reduces the risks of inflation, and hence cuts interest-rate costs. The credibility of Europe's monetary institutions is already greater, as we have seen, than that of its American counterparts. Governments whose countries are participating in Euroland are already able to borrow on better terms over a ten-year period than the American government, owing to the markets' belief that inflation is less likely to erode the value of the debt. If Britain joined the government would be able to reap substantial interest savings over time. Borrowers would also benefit from the reduction in interest costs, which could be as much as £142 a month for the average mortgage payer.

Most importantly for our longer-term prospects, businesses should find capital more easily and cheaply. Banks will compete fiercely for new business, and the new capital markets of the euro area are likely to encourage the growth of risk capital, particularly in the bond market. These interest rates and financial-market effects will help to reduce the cost of capital, and therefore boost investment. Lastly, the advent of a new world currency will offer Europeans the advantage of seignorage: the ability to buy other people's exports and offer them printed bank-notes in exchange. The euro is likely to become a major world currency, used as a store of value, a means of exchange and a unit of account much beyond Euroland.

These general advantages are reinforced by two particular features of Britain's situation, which mean that we may disproportionately benefit from the single currency. The first is our ability to attract foreign direct investment (FDI). If we join this will be underpinned. Indeed, we may benefit from the new wave of investment likely in the early years of EMU. The second is the position of the City of London as Europe's incipient financial centre. Within EMU London can be more than just a centre of international finance. It can be the centre of the new, integrated euro capital markets. Outside EMU not only is our share of FDI likely to dwindle, at particular cost to some of our poorer regions, but also the City's role is likely to come under increasing challenge from Paris and Frankfurt.

These unique British factors, the importance of FDI and of the City, are part of the answer to the questions: Why not wait and see how things turn out? Why not wait until after the next election (as the Labour government suggests) or even until after the election after that (as the Conservatives suggest)? What, after all, could be more reasonable? EMU has gone ahead with a large membership. The great experiment has begun. But if we wait we also increase the risk of losses because foreign investors go elsewhere, and because other centres pick up business from the City. Nor are we likely to settle the issue by waiting. The sorts of things that might go wrong with EMU, as we have seen, are unlikely to happen quickly. They might never happen. They might happen only after 20 years. No one is really suggesting that we can wait that long. Even the 'doctrine of unripe time', that famous bureaucratic delaying tactic when arguments of principle fail or prove inexpedient, would not sustain British non-membership for such a period. The government is already worried about the loss of political influence within Europe entailed by Britain's non-membership in such an important European project.

There is another point about delay. If something creates serious strains within EMU the odds are that it will be fixed. The show will go on. This is the experience of the European Union to date, particularly with big projects such as EMU in which so much political capital has been invested. If we are out, we will not have the problems. But we will not be part of the solutions either. This will bring potential economic and political costs as well. Indeed, even a temporary delay could be used against Britain, as the delay in our initial membership of the European Union was used to put in place policies for agriculture and fisheries which were inimical to British interests. There is a risk that

Britain, outside EMU, could be 'De Gaulled' again while Paris and Frankfurt benefit at the expense of the City, and the Pas de Calais benefits at the expense of South Wales and the North-west in the race for Japanese and American investment. Far from being at the heart of European affairs, we could become as uncomfortably marginal as we felt in the 1960s. As Professor Willem Buiter, a member of the Bank of England's Monetary Policy Committee, has said, 'Until the United Kingdom is a member of EMU, it will have second fiddle status in the concert of Europe.'

If you believe, as most British people seem to believe according to the opinion polls, that British membership of the euro is merely a matter of time, then it is supremely irrational to delay. We will, as we have seen, learn nothing from a delay on the sort of timescale that people suggest. Our interest rates have begun the long convergence process, and both our economic slowdown and lower interest rates will create an opportunity to lock into the euro soon. We will, when we join, have to pay all the upfront costs (such as conversion costs for slot machines) in any case. But with each month that passes we are delaying the benefits. If an investment is worth undertaking, it is worth undertaking as soon as possible so as to bring the benefits on stream as soon as possible. British membership of EMU is precisely such a case. We will make the investment before long, so it makes no sense to delay the benefits. Nor does it make any sense to risk increasing the costs by prolonging our self-imposed period of political impotence. Time and again Britain has delayed participation in Europe-wide projects which our partners have deemed to be essential. We continue to pay the price for these delays in both the Common Agricultural Policy and the Common Fisheries Policy. How long must we go on doing so on this occasion?

The Eurosceptics increasingly recognise the power of this logic as they flail to find an alternative vision for Britain and its economy in the 21st century. This is one reason Conrad Black, the Canadian proprietor of the *Telegraph* newspapers, recently wrote an interesting article in his own journal, entitled 'Britain's final choice: Europe or America?', which rather let the cat out of the bag.[54] Mr Black argued that Britain should leave the European Union and become a member of the North American Free Trade Agreement (NAFTA). 'If the United States received a signal from a British government that it wished to avail itself of a North American option, they would respond immediately,' he wrote. 'If America were jubilant, Canada would be ecstatic.' So there is a secret agenda, but is not on the part of the pro-Europeans; it is the secret agenda of the anti-Europeans, which is to leave the European Union.

This is, of course, a rich newspaper proprietor's whimsy since the Americans have pushed hardest for British membership of the European Union, and take British views seriously in exact proportion to our influence in Europe. Leaving aside the other small question of geography, or perhaps oceanography, the problem for most British people with Mr Black's vision is that we have no more desire to become an appendage of the United States than to be subsumed into a European superstate. The European Union, with all its cultural, social and ethnic diversity, suits British interests well. Yet we cannot long stand aside from the central project of the European Union, already adopted by 11 other member states and soon to be adopted by many others.

The euro is a big change, but it has come to seem a much smaller one in the context of present hyperactive international markets. Do we want to live in a world where exchange rates can be so buffeted by speculation that they can move by nearly 10% in one trading session, and where the reasonable expectations of our exporters can be overturned in a week? Lord Keynes warned that the financial system should never allow the bubbles and froth of speculation to undermine the steady efforts of commerce and industry. He was right. We need to use our sovereignty to provide a stable environment for our businesses, in the same way that we have rightly used our sovereignty to provide a secure defence within NATO. What sort of freedom is it to hike interest rates so high to defend your exchange rate that you drive the economy into recession? Our present financial system is not sustainable. We can move back to a world where free movement of capital and even of trade come increasingly into question. Or we can ensure the benefits of greater international integration by adopting the euro. In a real world of hard choices, the pound's days are numbered. The euro is our future.

Notes

1   Flora, Kraus and Pfenning (1987).
2   See Giavazzi and Giovannini (1989) for an analysis of exchange-rate policy in Europe, including the formation of the European Monetary System.
3   Several academics made the argument and so did the European Commission in *One market, one money*. Some economic commentators had also pointed out this problem, including the author in an article in *The Independent* shortly before the break-up.
4   Bureau Européen des Unions de Consommateurs (1988).
5   European Commission (1990).
6   Engel and Rogers (1996).
7   Baldwin (1990). See Emerson and Huhne (1991) for a discussion of these effects.
8   European Commission (1990).
9   See Thygesen (1998); Gros and Thygesen (1998).
10 This point relies heavily on Baldwin (1989 and 1990).
11 KPMG (1997).
12 The Council of Mortgage Lenders estimates that the average outstanding mortgage in mid-1998 was £40,000. The average new advance, however, was much higher at £55,000.
13 European Commission (1990).
14 Median earnings of men and women at full-time adult rates in April 1997 were £19,115 according to the New Earnings Survey.
15 See Porter and Judson (1996).
16 Mundell (1998).
17 IMF (1997).
18 See Fatas (1998).

19 Hummels, Rapoport and Yi (1998).

20 Bank for International Settlements cited in Dornbusch, Favero and Giavazzi (1998).

21 See Ramaswamy and Sloek (1997).

22 Dornbusch, Favero and Giavazzi (1998).

23 See Sachs and Sala-I-Martin (1992), who estimated 30–40% of the original fall in income is compensated; Bayoumi and Masson (1996) estimate a net effect of 30%.

24 See Fatas (1998). This result is also similar to Von Hagen (1992).

25 Fatas (1998).

26 The Stability and Growth Pact is set out in Council Regulations 1466/97 and 1467/97.

27 This broad conclusion is supported by all the studies known to the author on this subject, including the IMF's usual structural budget balance measures. A different methodology used by researchers at the Austrian National Bank comes to the same conclusion. See Brandner, Diepalek and Schuberth (1998).

28 Currie (1997).

29 Thygesen (1998).

30 Emerson and Huhne (1991).

31 See Vinals and Jimeno (1996). See also the estimates in Layard, Nickell and Jackman (1991).

32 Nickell (1997).

33 There is a useful discussion of the key features of the 'Rhineland' model in Davidson (1998).

34 Andersen Consulting (1998), from UNCTAD data.

35 JETRO data.

36 Andersen Consulting (1998), from Eurostat.

37 Centre for Economic and Business Research (1992).

38 See Andersen Consulting (1998), page 22.

39 See Szymanski (1994).

40 These figures are drawn from the study conducted by the Centre for Economic and Business Research (1998) for the Corporation

of London.

41 Ibid.

42 Ibid.

43 See Bank for International Settlements, Annual Report, 1998, Basle, page 84.

44 See, for example, John Redwood (1997).

45 *European Economy*, No. 63, 1997.

46 Quoted by the Social Security Committee of the House of Commons, October 1996.

47 A useful discussion of these issues is found in Arrowsmith, Barrell and Taylor (1998).

48 See, for example, Arrowsmith ed. (1998).

49 See, for example, Eichengreen and Wyplosz (1998).

50 Fatas (1998).

51 Commission of the European Communities (1977).

52 See also Sir Donald MacDougall's subsequent discussion of the report of the study group; MacDougall (1992).

53 For a clear assessment of the options, including what needs to happen if we stay out of the euro, see the report of an independent panel chaired by Rupert Pennant-Rea, CEPR (1997).

54 Extracts from 'Britain's final choice: Europe or America?', a speech by Conrad Black at the annual meeting of the Centre for Policy Studies, *Daily Telegraph*, July 10th 1998.

References

Alberola, E. and Tyrvainen, T. (1998) 'Is there scope for inflation differentials in EMU? An empirical evaluation of the Balassa-Samuelson model in EMU countries', Discussion Papers, 15, Economics Department, Bank of Finland.

Andersen Consulting (1998) *Business, Britain and Europe: the first 25 years*, European Movement, London.

Arrowsmith, J. (1998, July) 'Large scale EMU: the May council decisions and implications for monetary policy', *National Institute Economic Review*, London.

Arrowsmith, J. (ed.) (1998) 'Thinking the unthinkable about EMU: coping with turbulence between 1998 and 2002', National Institute Occasional Paper No. 51, London.

Arrowsmith, J., Barrell, R. and Taylor, C. (1998, October) 'Managing the Euro in a Tri-polar World', paper presented at the 21st colloquium of the Société Universitaire Européene de Recherches Financières, Frankfurt (mimeo).

Balassa, B. (1964, December) 'The Purchasing Power Parity doctrine: a reappraisal', *Journal of Political Economy*.

Baldwin, R. (1989, October) 'The growth effects of 1992', *Economic Policy*.

Baldwin, R. (1990) 'On the microeconomics of EMU', in Commission of the European Communities, *One Market, One Money*.

Bayoumi, T. (1989, August), 'Saving Investment correlations: immobile capital, government policy or endogenous behaviour?', IMF Working Paper No. 89/66.

Bayoumi, T. and Masson, P.R. (1996) 'Fiscal flows in the United

States and Canada: Lessons for monetary union in Europe', *European Economic Review*.

Brandner, P., Diepalek, L. and Schuberth, H. (1998) 'Structural budget deficits and sustainability of fiscal positions in the European Union', Working Paper No. 26, Oesterreichische NationalBank, Vienna.

Bureau Européen des Unions de Consommateurs (BEUC) (April, 1988) *Transferts de l'Argent a l'intérieur de la CEE*.

Canzoneri, M., Diba, B. and Eudey, G. (1996, June) 'Trends in European productivity and real exchange rates: implications for the Maastricht convergence criteria and for inflation targets after EMU', Centre for Economic Policy Research, Discussion Paper No. 1417.

Centre for Economics and Business Research for the Confederation of British Industry (1992) *The impact of UK attitudes to the EU on inward investment into the UK*.

Centre for Economics and Business Research for the Corporation of London (1998) *The City's Importance to the European Union Economy*.

Commission of the European Communities (1977, April) *Report of the Study Group on the role of Public Finance in European Integration* (The MacDougall report), Brussels.

Currie, D. (1997) *The pros and cons of EMU*, Economist Intelligence Unit, London.

Davidson, I. (1998) *Jobs and the Rhineland Model*, Federal Trust.

Deutsch, R. (1998, January) *The advent of a true euro corporate and high yield market*, Merrill Lynch.

Dornbusch, R., Favero, C. and Giavazzi, F. (1998, April) 'Immediate challenges for the European Central Bank', *Economic Policy*, No. 26.

Eichengreen, B. (1996, December) 'EMU: an outsider's perspective', Center for International and Development Economics Research (CIDER), Working Paper No. C96-079, University of California, Berkeley.

Eichengreen, B. and Wyplosz, C. (1998, April) 'The Stability Pact: more than a minor nuisance?', *Economic Policy*.

Emerson, M. and Huhne, C. (1991) *The Ecu report*, London.

Emerson, M., Aujean, M., Catinat, M., Goybet P. and Jacquemin A. (1988) *The Economics of 1992*, OUP, Oxford.

Emerson, M., Gros, C., Italianer A., Pisani-Ferry J. and Reichenbach H. (1992) *One Market, One Money*, OUP, Oxford.

Engel, C. and Rogers, J.H. (1996, December) 'How wide is the border?', *American Economic Review*.

European Commission (1990, October) 'One Market, One Money', *European Economy*, No. 44, Luxembourg.

European Commission (1998) *Infeuro Newsletter*, No. 8.

Fatas, A. (1998, April) 'Does EMU need a fiscal federation?', INSEAD Working Paper, *Economic Policy*, No. 26.

Fatas, A. (1997, January) 'EMU countries or regions? Lessons from the EMS experience', *European Economic Review*, Vol. 41.

Feldstein, M. (1977) *Foreign Affairs,* Vol. 76, No. 6, pages 60–73.

Flora, P., Kraus, F. and Pfenning, W. (1987) *State, Economy and Society in Western Europe, 1815–1975*, two volumes, London.

Forder, J. (1998a) 'The case for an independent European Central Bank: A reassessment of evidence and sources', *European Journal of Political Economy*, Vol. 14, pages 53–72.

Forder, J. (1998b) 'Central Bank Independence – Conceptual Clarifications and Interim Assessment', *Oxford Economic Papers*, Vol. 50, pages 307–334.

Forder, J. (1998c) 'Is the European Union really a Friend of Free Trade?', Politeia Lecture, December 15th 1998.

Friedman, M. (1968) 'The role of monetary policy', *American Economic Review*, pages 1–17.

Giavazzi, F. and Giovannini, A. (1989) *Limiting exchange rate flexibility: the European Monetary System*, MIT press, Cambridge, MA.

Gros, D. and Thygesen, N. (1991) *European Monetary Integration*, Longman, London.

Gros, D. and Thygesen, N. (1998) *European Monetary Integration: From the EMS to EMU*, London and New York.

Hummels, D., Rapoport, D. and Yi, Kei-Mu (1998, June) 'Vertical specialisation and the changing nature of world trade', *Economic Policy Review*, Vol. 4, No. 2, Federal Reserve Bank of New York.

IMF (1997, October) *World Economic Outlook*.

Johnson, C. (1996) *In with the Euro, out with the pound: the single currency for Britain*, London.

KPMG Management Consulting (1997) 'Europe's preparedness for EMU', Research Report.

Layard, R., Nickell, S. and Jackman, R. (1991) *Unemployment: macroeconomic performance and the labour market*, Oxford.

MacDougall, Sir D. (1992, May) 'Economic and Monetary Union and the European Community budget', *National Institute Economic Review*, National Institute of Economic and Social Research.

Mazower, M. (1998) *Dark Continent: Europe's twentieth century*, London.

Milesi, G. (1998) *Le Roman de l'Euro*, Paris.

Mundell, R. (1998, March 24th) 'Great Expectations for the Euro', *Wall Street Journal Europe*.

Nickell, S. (1997) 'Unemployment and Labour Market Rigidities: Europe versus North America', *Journal of Economic Perspectives*, Vol. 11, No. 3.

OECD (1994) *Country report on France*, Paris.

OECD (1995) *Country report on France*, Paris.

OECD (1997) *Country report on France*, Paris.

OECD (1998) *OECD Economic Outlook*.

Oppenheimer, P. and Forder J. (1996) 'The Changing Rationale of Monetary Union' in Hayward, J. (ed) *Elitism, Populism and European Politics*, OUP, Oxford.

Pennant-Rea, R. *et al.* (1997) *The Ostrich and the EMU: policy choices facing the United Kingdom*, Centre for Economic Policy Research, London.

Porter, R.D. and Judson, R.A. (1996, October) 'The location of US currency: how much of it is abroad?', *Federal Reserve Bulletin*, Vol. 82.

Ramaswamy, R. and Sloek, T. (1997, December) 'The real effects of monetary policy in the European Union: what are the differences?', International Monetary Fund Working Paper WP/97/160.

Redwood, J. (1997) *Our currency, our country: the dangers of European Monetary Union*, London.

Sachs, J. and Sala-I-Martin, X. (1992) 'Fiscal Federalism and Optimum currency areas: evidence from Europe and the United States', in Canzoneri, M., Grilli, V. and Masson, P. (eds) *Establishing a Central Bank: issues in Europe and lessons from the US*.

Samuelson, P. (1964, May) 'Theoretical notes on trade problems', *Review of Economics and Statistics*.

Szymanski, S. (1994, September) 'The City Labour market', in *The City Research Project*, Corporation of London.

Thygesen, N. (1998, May) 'EMU, Britain and other outsiders', Special Paper No. 102, Financial Markets Group, London School of Economics.

Vinals, J. and Jimeno, J.F. 'Monetary Union and European Unemployment', Documento de Trabajo No. 9624, Servicio de Estudios, Banco de Espana.

Von Hagen, J. (1992) 'Fiscal Arrangements in a monetary union: evidence from the US', in Fair, S. and de Boissieu, C. (eds) *Fiscal Policy, Taxes and the Financial System in an Increasingly Integrated Europe*, Kluwer, Dordrecht.

Index

F refers to the page numbers in the 'For' book and **A** refers to page numbers in the 'Against' book.